CAROL VINCENT

TEA AND THE QUEEN?

Fundamental British Values, Schools
and Citizenship

POLICY PRESS SHORTS RESEARCH

First published in Great Britain in 2019 by

Policy Press
University of Bristol
1-9 Old Park Hill
Bristol
BS2 8BB
UK
t: +44 (0)117 954 5940
pp-info@bristol.ac.uk
www.policypress.co.uk

North America office:
Policy Press
c/o The University of Chicago Press
1427 East 60th Street
Chicago, IL 60637, USA
t: +1 773 702 7700
f: +1 773 702 9756
sales@press.uchicago.edu
www.press.uchicago.edu

British Library Cataloguing in Publication Data
A catalogue record for this book is available from the British Library.

Library of Congress Cataloging-in-Publication Data
A catalog record for this book has been requested.

ISBN 978-1-4473-5195-5 (hardback)
ISBN 978-1-4473-5197-9 (ePub)
ISBN 978-1-4473-5196-2 (ePDF)

The right of Carol Vincent to be identified as author of this work has been asserted by her in accordance with the Copyright, Designs and Patents Act 1988.

Cover design by blu inc, Bristol
Front cover: image kindly supplied by iStock
Printed and bound in Great Britain by CPI Group (UK) Ltd,
Croydon, CR0 4YY
Policy Press uses environmentally responsible print partners

This book is dedicated to the memory of Wendy Ball who, sadly, passed away in December 2018 while I was finishing this book. A friend from our days as new academics, she was thoughtful, supportive and dedicated, qualities which were reflected in her academic work. She is much missed.

Contents

List of abbreviations

DfE	Department for Education
FBV	'fundamental British values'
GCE	global citizenship education
LGBT+	lesbian, gay, bisexual, transgender/transsexual and other groups
MAT	multi-academy trust
MHCLG	Ministry of Housing, Communities and Local Governance
Ofsted	Office for Standards in Education, Children's Services and Skills
PSHE	Personal, Social, Health and Economic education
QCA	Qualifications and Curriculum Authority
RSE	relationships and sex education (renamed by the government from SRE)
SMSC	spiritual, moral, social and cultural development
SRE	sex and relationships education

Acknowledgements

The research on which this book is based was funded by the Leverhulme Trust as a Major Research Fellowship (Award number: MRF-2015-170, October 2016–September 2018). I am very grateful to the trust for their support.

I owe a major debt of gratitude to the teachers who gave up their limited time to speak with me about fundamental British values. I came away from visiting their schools impressed by their dedication, thoughtfulness and determination. Having previously been a primary school teacher in London, I am acutely aware of how much more pressurised teaching is now as a result of the multiple demands made upon the profession. I hope I have given some sense of the complexity of teachers' working lives here.

I am used to working in research teams, so doing a solo project was an experience I haven't had since completing my PhD. One drawback is that there are no team members to discuss the research with as it unfolds, so I am particularly grateful to my much valued friends and colleagues who patiently provided a sounding board and lots of support. The project advisory group – Patrick Bailey, Doug Bourne, Alice Bradbury, Annette Braun, Christine Callender and James Wright – offered thoughtful comments and suggestions. Annette Braun, Alice Bradbury, Stephen Ball and Hugh Starkey kindly read draft chapters and gave me invaluable advice. Patrick Bailey competently took over my teaching and admin for the period of the fellowship and discussed character education with me. Bronwen Jones provided vital assistance in putting together a booklet listing resources on teaching political and social issues. Reza Gholami, Jonathan James and Andreas Pantelides contributed to a dissemination event for this project, and in doing so made it much more rounded and comprehensive than it would otherwise have been. Margaret Leggett, who has valiantly stuck with many of my research projects over the years, competently and reliably – as always – transcribed the interviews. Friends and family outside academia also showed an unflagging and much appreciated interest in the research. Michele Harrison, Elizabeth Hess and my siblings, Dave Hibbin and Anne Hallitt, deserve a particular mention. As usual, my husband, Ian, and (now alarmingly grown-up) children, Madi and Dan, provide the strongest grounding in my life and remind me that there is much more to life than academic work! To them, as ever, all my love and thanks.

This book is partially based on material in two previous papers published in *Theory and Research in Education* and the *British Journal of Sociology of Education*. All material has been fully revised and elaborated for this book.

Introduction: the promotion of fundamental British values

Year 9 class (13/14 year olds) in a Religion and Ethics lesson. The class are mainly White, with one Black child. On the smart board is a question: "What 5 words would you use to describe 'British' or 'British values'?" The teacher explains the difference between things we would think of as 'British' and values which are 'what do we stand for?' The feedback for 'British' includes: posh people, fish and chips, crumpets, Empire, Wallace and Gromit [hapless cartoon characters], Harrods [an expensive department store], cricket, and discussion of the weather. The values include: education, monarchy, patriotism and being polite. (Field notes, Downs Secondary Academy, rural/suburban area, mixed class, mainly White British population)

Since 2014, teachers in all schools in England have been required to 'promote' the 'fundamental British values' of democracy, rule of law, individual liberty and mutual respect and tolerance of those of different faiths and beliefs. This book explores the response from teachers, drawing on data collected in 2016–17 from interviews with 56 teachers and other education professionals and from 49 observations of lessons, assemblies and workshops. The English schools' inspectorate, Ofsted (Office for Standards in Education, Children's Services and Skills), assess both how schools promote 'fundamental British values' (FBV) and how they prepare students for 'life in modern Britain' as part of their school inspections. From September 2019, schools will be required to 'develop [pupils'] understanding of' FBV as part of 'preparing pupils for life in modern Britain' (Ofsted, 2019 para 28). This slight change in wording may perhaps recognise some of the public criticisms of the requirement discussed later, but it is unlikely to impact significantly upon practice. The requirement to promote FBV falls on teachers in England in both the independent and the state-funded sectors, but not, at the time of writing, on those in Wales, Scotland or Northern Ireland because of their devolved education systems. The immediate confusion arising from that situation – promoting 'British' values only in English schools – also impacts the wider project: how do these identified values fit into a national narrative of Britishness? Indeed, what does and should constitute such a national narrative? People's reactions to those questions are shaped by their perceptions of increasing ethnic and religious diversity in the population.

Throughout this book, I discuss themes of nationalism, citizenship, cohesion and belonging. I focus on teachers' responses to the FBV requirement, and how these are influenced by their priorities and values, as well as by the immediate institutional context and the wider social and political climate in which they work. I am interested in the 'technologies of governmentality' (Fortier, 2016: 1040) deployed by both schools and the state to define a 'good' citizen, and in how feelings around belonging to the school and to the nation are mobilised and interpreted by teachers.

The structure of the book is as follows: Chapter One considers the social and political contexts of the FBV requirement, as I argue that the enactment of particular policies cannot be understood without reference to the broader climate, what Ball (1994) calls 'the context of influence'. Chapter Two explores some of the vast literature around citizenship and nationalism, focusing on what Conversi refers to as the 'deliberate cultivation of common [national] allegiances' (2014: 28) and the role of universal democratic principles in so doing. I draw attention to the arguments of several commentators that asserting a national identity through commitment to apparently universal liberal democratic principles often obscures the existence of narrower cultural and ethnic understandings of belonging. Chapter Two also considers the role of citizenship education in promoting national and global belonging, and identifies some of the recent developments in the subject in England and elsewhere. I also focus briefly on the impact of counter-extremism policies in education. Chapter Three discusses the processes of 'policy enactment' (Ball et al, 2012), outlines the education policy context and introduces the schools involved in this research. Chapters Four and Five describe and analyse the four main school responses to the promotion of FBV that I identified: *Representing Britain*, *Repackaging FBV*, *Relocating FBV* and *Engagement with FBV*. *Representing Britain* describes the use of symbols and stereotypes traditionally associated with Britain as a mechanism through which to promote FBV. *Repackaging* describes a business-as-usual response whereby schools absorb the promotion of FBV into their existing practices. *Relocating* describes the rise in 'inward-looking' values/character education. I argue that this emphasis on personal development is preferred over more 'outward-looking' citizenship education. *Engagement* (in Chapter Five) considers the more infrequent instances of direct engagement with FBV in schools, including teachers' incursions into controversial/sensitive issues. Chapter Five also explores the priorities of teacher-respondents, their interpretation of the FBV policy to fit with their emphasis on developing students' moral behaviours, and the commonalities and differences across the schools in the research, in terms of how 'useful' staff understood the FBV requirement to be in relation to their student populations. Chapter Six concludes the book by summarising its themes and considering the definition and role of critical citizenship education. I conclude that the FBV is a deeply flawed project. In order to allow for maximum consensus, the values are rarely examined and defined, acting instead as a form of ideological comfort food, an assertion of Britain's occupation of the moral high ground.

The data in the book address the specifics of the English situation. However, the broader issues – discussion of the processes of policy enactment, nationalism, national identity and belonging, and the use of schools and teachers to disseminate supposedly national values and to play a role in government counter-extremism agendas – are relevant to a wider international audience. Within the current context of population mobility, and heightened anxiety about and hostility towards migrants, the resurgence of the far right and the growth of populism in Europe, the US and other countries around the world, debates around nation, cohesion and citizenship retain a fundamental importance.

ONE

'Managing' diversity: policy and practice

> One of democracy's strictest tests [is] the challenge to work
> and live with and share not just with people with whom we
> have a great deal in common, but also those with whom
> we happen to be bound up. (Honig, 2001: 117–18)

This chapter opens with Bonnie Honig's discussion of how
attitudes towards 'the foreigner' contain both welcome and
celebration (xenophilia) and fear and hatred (xenophobia).
I illustrate my argument for a contemporary tilt towards
xenophobia by reviewing the shift in the English policy
landscape from multiculturalism to cohesion, along with the
growth of anti-extremist policies. I then locate the requirement
to promote FBV within this increasingly illiberal landscape.

The nation and the 'other': belonging in 21st-century Britain

The American political philosopher Bonnie Honig argues that
'solving' 'the problems of foreignness' underlies contemporary
discussions of democracy and citizenship (2001: 1), and
that attitudes towards 'the foreigner' are shot through with
ambivalence.[1] The foreigner is both a potential threat and a

potential saviour. Honig uses examples from US literature and film to make her case, but I give an example here from Shakespeare (as studying his work was sometimes offered as evidence of promoting FBV: see Chapter Four). Fortinbras, prince of Norway, in *Hamlet*, appears in the final moment of the play on a stage filled with the dead bodies of the play's protagonists, to stabilise the collapsing state of Denmark. Most immigrants do not become the ruler of their new nation, of course, but Honig argues that the 'good' immigrant on a trajectory to citizenship will make the kind of explicit connection and commitment to the state (through citizenship ceremonies, for example) that the native-born population do not, thus further legitimising and energising the consent basis of the state. However, the shadow of the 'bad' immigrant – an illegal alien – remains potent. Since Honig was writing, the 'haphazard' balance (Kofman, 2005: 461) between xenophobia and xenophilia – which Honig understood as a 'co-presence' (2001: 97) – has surely shifted towards xenophobia in both the UK and the US. The illegality of the alien and their illegitimate consumption of a nation-state's resources is now sketched in lurid tabloid colours as migration from both Eastern Europe and poor and war-torn parts of Africa and the Middle East has continued. Particularly since 9/11 and the 2007 terrorist attacks in London, an additional shadow posed by the alien has come to the fore – a sense of threat to 'our' way of life from migrant populations – or populations with migrant heritage – positioned as not sharing 'our' values and not wishing to integrate. However, another narrative – although one that is flimsier and more fragile – also persists of Britain as a country with a long multiethnic history, at ease with diversity. In recent years, the London 2012 Olympics, the marriage of biracial Meghan Markle into the Royal Family and the multiracial England football team at the 2018 World Cup have all been presented (at least in the liberal media) as evidence of a country open to and comfortable with ethnic difference.[2] Additionally, sociological research on 'encounters' and 'everyday multiculturalism' has argued that many inhabitants of highly diverse areas demonstrate a largely metropolitan competence with and acceptance of difference in everyday life (see Neal et al, 2018 for review). Within the metropolitan middle classes, this is often presented as a perhaps rather self-conscious impulse to appreciate diversity, to have smooth relationships with those who are different, to avoid prejudice or intolerance, to conform to what Ahmed (2014) refers to as the 'imperative to love difference' (although this desire may not translate into close friendships, e.g. Jackson and Benson, 2014; Vincent, Neal and Iqbal, 2018). The next section discusses the tilt towards xenophobia, while not forgetting this impulse – unevenly distributed, perhaps, across people and places – that seeks to welcome diversity.

The context for FBV

The enactment of any particular policy cannot be understood without an awareness of the context in which it is being formulated and put into practice. Any brief account risks elision, inaccuracy and loss of nuance; yet, with those risks in mind, I want to identify some aspects of the historical and contemporary context to the requirement to promote FBV in schools (see also Revell and Bryan, 2018).

The entanglement of contemporary talk of 'British values' with Britain's past is hard to ignore. Writing on the British empire and its various phases of expansion and contraction is vast and much debated, but I want to acknowledge here the background consciousness provided by the existence of the empire to contemporary discussions of citizenship, ethnic and racial diversity, and values. 'Empire', says Bayley, 'must be seen not only as a critical phase in the history of the Americas, Asia or Africa but in the very creation of British nationalism itself' (1989: 15). Bayley talks about the period 1780–1830 as witnessing the 'expansion of British dominion, of techniques of governance and exploitation' (p. 2) underpinned by beliefs in free trade, hierarchies based on race, 'true' religion and 'uniform notions of "law" and "progress"' (p. 14). Arguably, and despite contemporary notions of equality, these imperial values still echo in contemporary debates and practices surrounding 'British values'.

Additionally, the context of the policy's formulation and of school responses is shaped by several current factors. These include the changing political rhetoric around responses to difference signalled in the varying use of the terms 'multiculturalism', 'cohesion' and 'integration' (which are further discussed later). Throughout this century, New Labour and Conservative politicians have all been eager to pronounce on 'Britishness'.[3] A proposal to teach 'traditional British values' in schools was first mooted in 2006 by a New Labour government minister, Bill Rammell, a proposal finally enacted by Michael Gove, a Conservative government minister eight years later, in 2014.

Other important aspects of the contemporary climate include the anti-extremist Prevent policy, the 2016 referendum on leaving the European Union, and government citizenship policy. The Prevent policy, part of a series of policies which make up CONTEST, the government's counter-terrorism strategy, is inextricably linked with the promotion of FBV as discussed later in this chapter. The full result of the 2016 decision to leave the European Union is still not clear at the time of writing, but it seems that in some areas the decision to vote to leave the EU was a crystallisation of public alarm at and hostility over immigration (Goodwin and Milazzo, 2017). Home Office figures for 2017–18 show a rise in recorded hate crimes in England and Wales after the 2016 referendum and the 2017 terror attacks, to the extent that hate crimes have doubled in the last five years (National Police Chiefs' Council, 2017; O'Neill, 2017; Home Office, 2018b). The tightening of citizenship regulations through, for example, the Home Office's policy of creating a 'hostile environment'[4] for immigrants, and mandatory and expensive citizenship tests are designed to reassure 'the "neurotic citizen" (Isin, 2004) that the boundaries around the nation and who is to be considered a member of the nation are sufficiently high and arduous' (Byrne, 2016: 12; see also Tyler, 2010; Banks, 2017).

From 'state multiculturalism' to 'cohesion' and 'integration'

In this section, I focus on changing policy terminology about 'managing' a multiethnic population. Language in this area is fluid: terms are often not closely defined but are used and perceived in shifting, malleable ways. I discuss the policy drift away from 'multiculturalism' towards 'cohesion'. It is important to state here that language that seeks to challenge power relations at the heart of race and ethnic inequalities, such as anti-racism and, more recently, White privilege,[5] has been and is largely confined to the academy and to a small number of local authorities, schools and activists. The widely-used, current terminology of 'diversity' and 'equalities' has been criticised for decentring race and ethnicity, instituting instead a broad range of issues and raising concerns about the diluting of policy responses[6] (Lewis and Craig, 2014).

In the last few decades of the twentieth century, multiculturalism became a relatively accepted government approach to diversity, albeit one that was accepted more at local than at central government level. A multicultural approach means, broadly, that ethnic, linguistic and religious diversity within a nation is recognised, welcomed and even celebrated in policy and that adaptations may be made for specific groups (see Modood, 2013 and Bulmer and Solomos 2017 for discussion). It is an approach that challenges liberal universalism. Multicultural approaches in schools have largely meant the inclusion of artefacts and curriculum content reflecting a range of multiethnic groups, incorporating different languages and recognising different religious practices. Much of this remains standard practice in the schools I observed, especially those with multiethnic populations.

However, the emphasis of government policy began to change in the early years of this century following 9/11, the 2005 London Transport terror attacks and urban disturbances in the north of England in 2001. The emphasis moved towards cohesion, not just in England but in a range of European states (Colombo, 2015) as the argument that multiculturalism 'foster[ed] the creation of bounded enclaves' (Kostakopoulou, 2010 : 936) grew in prominence (for a rebuttal of this view, see Mason, 2018). As Suvarierol comments, 'Discussions on national norms and values, historical blueprints, the national flag and anthem are hot issues in Europe again' (2012: 210). Joppke (2007) notes the turn in many European states over this period towards 'civic integration', meaning the *obligatory* integration of newcomers into participation in mainstream institutions. Citizenship instruction and tests are now widespread. These developments can be understood as part of a wider embrace of neoconservative policies that 'glorif[y] a particular vision of the past associated with the dominant group and its understanding of traditional values' (Joshee and Sinfield, 2010: 61). In 2011 the then prime minister David Cameron famously declared that 'Under the doctrine of state multiculturalism, we have encouraged different cultures to live separate lives, apart from each other and apart from the mainstream'. He called for a stronger feeling of belonging to local communities which would lead to a 'true cohesion'. He also called for a 'muscular liberalism' which would assert the particular values of the nation:

I believe a genuinely liberal country does much more [than passively tolerate difference]; it believes in certain values and actively promotes them. Freedom of speech, freedom of worship, democracy, the rule of law, equal rights regardless of race, sex or sexuality. It says to its citizens, this is what defines us as a society: to belong here is to believe in these things. Now, each of us in our own countries, I believe, must be unambiguous and hard-nosed about this defence of our liberty. (Cameron, 2011)

This narrative of multiculturalism presents it as a failed ideology which has resulted in segregation, isolation, an absence of integration, with minority communities who refuse to adopt 'our' values. Multiculturalism, in this reading, is assumed to result in minority groups imposing their unreasonable demands despite the concerns of the majority, and abusing the tolerance of that majority. Their difference apparently threatens the integrity, safety and security of England and other Western European nations. Value sharing is understood as indicative of harmony but value difference as grounds for conflict (Edyvane, 2011). Lentin (2014) argues that this critique of multiculturalism is not in essence merely a critique of the policy landscape, but rather of the very *presence* of those who bring racial, ethnic and/ or cultural diversity to the country. Following Barker's (1981) separation of 'new' cultural racism and 'old' biological racism, Lentin continues that 'culture' has become the sphere in which difference is marked, in part at least because of the taboo around overt racism. Thus 'the furore over multiculturalism … is not separate from the story of racism; rather, it is its contemporary manifestation' (Lentin, 2014: 1273). This view, based on the idea that 'racial/cultural minorities have gained the upper hand, advocates for reinstating the hegemonic status (as if it were ever displaced) of the cultural/white majority' (p. 1280). This means countering 'their' excess with 'more of "our" culture; more "citizenship" events, nationalist commemorations and integration tests' (p. 1277). Thus, a space for the assertion of a set of national values is opened up.

The discrimination and economic inequalities experienced by many minority groups are absent in the anti-multiculturalism discourse. Also absent is the more complex story provided by research on 'everyday multiculturalism', mentioned earlier, which emphasises the possession of everyday skills, knowledges and competencies that are mobilised and enacted by people living in diverse localities in their interactions with 'others' (e.g. Vincent et al, 2018). This positive perception is at odds with policy narratives of differences in culture, ethnicity and religion, leading to inevitable fracture, segregation and isolation.

I am not asserting a 'golden age' of multiculturalism. Indeed, multiculturalism as a policy approach has long been an idea under attack, with challenges from the left as well as the already identified arguments from the right. I note three arguments from the left here. First, multiculturalism in education and elsewhere in public policy has been criticised for being tokenistic, for focusing on colour, spectacle and exoticism and for not addressing the roots of discrimination and prejudice (a strategy that does that would require a clear willingness to do what multiculturalism does not: name and challenge racism and the privileging of White identities (Troyna, 1993). Relatedly, multiculturalism rarely emphasises changing the attitudes of the White majority (Modood, 2013; Keddie, 2014). Second, it has been argued that the focus on culture avoids attention being paid to the socio-economic inequalities experienced by many minoritised groups (e.g. Joppke, 2004). Third, multiculturalism has also been criticised for taking on a neoliberal form, exemplified by the advertising strategy of the Benetton clothing company, which features harmonious groups of multiracial children and young people as a way of 'repackag[ing] cultural difference ... as a commodity or lifestyle good that can be marketed and consumed' (Kymlicka, 2007: 130).

To return to the retreat from multiculturalism that is visible in politicians' speeches in many western liberal states: despite this retreat, what Joppke (2004) calls 'difference-conscious' policies persist, which arguably have an influence on minimising value difference and emphasising cohesion (Korteweg and Triadafilopoulos, 2015. 'Diversity' in the form of colourful and exotic 'multicultural manifestations' (Joiko, 2019) persists in the UK and in so doing acts to illustrate the nation's tolerance (Kofman, 2005). Some commentators argue that multicultural policies on the ground have remained stable in many European countries including the UK (Banting and Kymlicka, 2017; Mathieu, 2018). To some extent, as will be seen, I agree with Mathieu (2018) who claims that multiculturalism in schools is resilient, especially those with a history of multiethnic populations. However, he arguably ignores several key elements of the current educational context, discussed in Chapter Three, and the demands on schools of counter-terrorism strategies.

Integration and cohesion

Kostakopulou (2010: 949) notes that the current policy impulse across many 'western' states retains the sense that diversity is 'somehow a threat and/or a problem' to a nation–state presented as otherwise organic, unified and homogeneous. This understanding underpins the stated need for immigrants to integrate[7] into the majority culture, and also informs some versions of 'community cohesion', a term which inserts the warm-glow word 'community' into discussions of relationships in places marked by difference and often disadvantage (Lewis and Craig, 2014: 23). After racial tension in northern English towns spilled onto the streets in 2001, an investigative team led by Ted Cantle argued that apparently multicultural areas were actually composed of monocultural settlements with Asian-heritage and White British populations living 'parallel lives', with little interaction. The report argued for community cohesion programmes that increased trust and respect 'by breaking down stereotypes and misconceptions about the "other"' (Cantle, 2019).

'Community cohesion', like 'multiculturalism', has become an amorphous term open to various interpretations and practices. The New Labour government (1997–2010) version reflected the influence of communitarianism, which emphasises cohesive communities possessed of a strong moral voice, committed to shared values and identity (see e.g. Etzioni, 1993). However, community cohesion policies do not necessarily assume minority assimilation, but 'seek to augment existing ethnic or social identities with common and overarching identities' (Thomas, 2011: 191). This understanding seeks to create rather than to impose forms of commonality (Cameron's speech, cited earlier, argues for imposition). Although Cantle claimed that both White and Asian residents in depressed Northern towns, the scene of the 2001 disturbances, were living 'parallel lives', the suspicion remained among commentators that some community cohesion policies were underpinned by a belief that particular groups were more in need of cohesion than others (Phillips, 2006; Lewis and Craig, 2014).

Some commentators prefer to use the term 'social cohesion', which draws in divisions based on social class (Green et al, 2009). Similarly, in a further proliferation of terminology, the London mayor, Sadiq Khan, launched a 'social integration' strategy in 2018. Social integration in this version centres (in)equality and 'the extent to which people positively interact and connect with others who are different to themselves. It is determined by the level of equality between people, the nature of their relationships, and their degree of participation in the communities in which they live' (Greater London Authority, 2018: 9). The malleability of all these terms is illustrated by a teacher in my research who commented that the issues now labelled as 'British values' on their curriculum had always been there but previously "might have been called, I don't know, multiculturalism".

Schools still retain a duty, originating in 2006, to promote 'community cohesion', but since 2011 the school inspectorate, Ofsted, is no longer required to report on this aspect. Research reports relating to this pre-2011 period argued that the Ofsted focus had led to an increase in teachers' activities around community cohesion (Phillips et al, 2011; Rowe et al, 2012). Both research teams also pointed to the differing definitions in play in schools, with community cohesion being variously defined as cutting across several issues such as 'citizenship, multiculturalism, faith and ethnicity' (Phillips et al, 2011: 8; see also Keating and Banton, 2013), with the ability to 'get along with' other people being a recurrent phrase (Rowe et al, 2012). However, today, 'community cohesion' appears to be outdated language. The pace of policy developments and initiatives in schools was such that, once the duty was removed from the Ofsted framework, the phrase was used infrequently. Indeed, for some of the younger teachers in my research, it was, as one said, "not really on my radar". This did not mean that the concern with developing students' sense of belonging and identity and their respect for others had disappeared, but it was no longer framed as 'community cohesion'. Previous policies, however, do not necessarily disappear without trace, and a history of initiatives around multiculturalism and community cohesion leave particular understandings and orientations – a policy 'sediment' (see Chapter Three), influencing existing work on 'equalities' and 'diversity'.

The Prevent strategy

The category of 'Muslims' is at the centre of the furore about responding to difference and diversity. Islam is, like other major religions, diverse, and has numerous adherents in countries with different histories, political and economic structures and social and cultural practices. However, the religion is often presented in homogenising and negative terms: as pre-modern and as intolerant, unbending and threatening to the liberal values put forward as a core constituent of European national identities (Morey and Yaquin, 2011). As a result, ' "Islam", "Islamic" and "Muslim" are in the contemporary climate … words that cannot be neutrally employed' (Allen, 2010: 196). Wesselhoeft comments that ' "Muslimness" has come to be seen as an ingrained and often corporeal essence of individuals from Muslim backgrounds … it has come to be understood as the most meaningful characteristic of those individuals, the primary lens through which their choices, views, and actions are to be understood' (2017: 627). As a result of this positioning, a discourse of 'conditional citizenship' appears applicable to Muslims and other minority groups (Cowden and Singh, 2017), a citizenship that has to be earned and deserved. Again, references to discrimination and socio-economic inequalities are silenced, although, as Cowden and Singh argue, 'anxieties about cohesion swim in a sea of material insecurity' (2017: 270).

The FBV requirement is deeply enmeshed with the government's anti-extremist policy Prevent. In 2015 the Prevent duty explicitly brought schools into the counter-extremist strategy by enshrining a legal responsibility on public bodies, including schools, to have 'due regard to the need to prevent people from being drawn into terrorism' (Counter-Terrorism and Security Act 2015, part 5, chapter 1, section 26). This meant that teachers had to undergo compulsory training in order to fulfil their duty to identify and report any colleagues or students displaying signs of being 'at risk' of 'being drawn into terrorism, including support for extremist ideas that are part of terrorist ideology'; 'extremism' is defined as 'vocal or active opposition to fundamental British values' (Home Office, 2015: 5). Those so suspected should be referred to the police-led multiagency Channel programme (for England and Wales) which provides intervention programmes and training for particular individuals.

Prevent is widely understood as a strategy to address a 'hidden threat' from potential terrorists born and raised in Britain (Tyler, 2010). Despite later versions invoking far right radicalisation in addition to Islamist extremism, it is still widely criticised for targeting and alienating Muslim communities and thus further deepening the demonisation of Muslims for their difference and presumed conservatism (Busher et al, 2017; Mac an Ghaill and Hayward, 2017; Thomas, 2017; Panjwani et al, 2018;

Joint Committee for Human Rights, 2017[8]). Thus, schools have been drawn into the securitisation matrix through the surveillance required by the Prevent duty, and the 'hearts and minds' promotion of British values in order to increase belonging and commitment to the nation-state. The teachers in my research had largely accepted the Prevent duty as part of their safeguarding responsibilities in line with government guidance[9] (Home Office, 2015; see also Busher et al, 2017), but others have voiced concerns about its potential impact on student–teacher trust (Ragazzi, 2017) and teacher autonomy and professionalism (Revell and Bryan, 2018), as well as the effects on Muslim communities of mistaken referrals to Prevent (Open Society Justice Initiative, 2016). Government figures show that the largest percentage of referrals to Prevent continue to relate to Islamist extremism (61 per cent in in the year to March 2017, but dropping to 44 per cent the following year, with a rise in right-wing extremism: Home Office, 2018a, 2018b). Thomas (2017) and O'Toole et al (2016) note differences in emphasis between central and local government, with some local governments trying to forestall existing community cohesion initiatives being coopted by Prevent, by integrating the two, to the extent that ground-level Prevent work may look significantly different to the overt surveillance of central government policy. O'Toole et al also argue that Prevent cannot be seen 'straightforwardly as a form of discipline given its contradictory, incoherent, and contested practice' (2016: 174). The same variation is likely to describe school reactions (Busher et al, 2017). The appointment of Prevent education officers in some local authorities has also created a further group of 'mid-level policy enactors' (Singh et al, 2013), attempting to mediate between central government agendas and what they understand to be the priorities on the ground. Thus, the role of the Prevent duty in contributing to the context for the promotion of particular national values cannot be underestimated. The continuing sense that all Muslims are potentially suspect persists, resulting in 2019 in a government announcement of a forthcoming independent review. Revell (2018) notes that the guidance to prevent radicalisation derives from a liberal agenda to foster agency (through building resilience in the vulnerable) and strengthen commitment to a democratic culture through cultivating mutual respect and tolerance. However, she also argues that

> These guidelines recommend pedagogies that model liberal qualities: debates, listening, reflection and questioning … They position themselves as liberal in opposition to the illiberalism of extremism. However, the claim to the liberal nature of these practices ignores the political context in which these resources are used and understood, where the content and aims of education are explicitly considered within a national security agenda. (Revell, 2018: 198)

The Equality Act 2010

Another relevant duty, infrequently mentioned in relation to FBV and Prevent, derives from the Equality Act 2010, according to which schools and teachers must have 'due regard to the need to eliminate discrimination, advance equality of opportunity and foster good relations between different people when carrying out their activities'.[10] It is unlawful for a school to discriminate against pupils by treating them less favourably because of their sex, race, disability, religion or belief, sexual orientation, gender reassignment, pregnancy or maternity (the ninth protected characteristic – age – does not apply to pupils). The Act is a British example of 'a liberal counterpoint to increasingly illiberal civic integration policies' (Joppke, 2007: 5). Although few teachers in this study referred specifically to the EqualityAct, its influence and the influence of previous equalities legislation can be traced in teacher–respondents' sense of what was clearly unacceptable in schools, such as racist name calling.

The Trojan Horse affair

By 2012, not 'undermining' British values already featured in the professional standards teachers have to adhere to in training in order to qualify. The immediate spur for the introduction of the requirement to promote FBV in schools was the Trojan Horse affair – the alleged 'infiltration' by extremist Muslims of state schools in Birmingham. In response, the then Secretary of State for Education, Michael Gove, pledged to 'put the promotion of British values at the heart of what every school has to deliver for children' (Hansard, 9 June 2014, col 266). The subject of four different investigations, the affair is difficult to unravel, but the 2015 report by the House of Commons Education Select Committee concluded that, with the exception of one incident, no evidence of extremism or radicalisation was found by any of the Trojan Horse inquiries, and in 2017 the charges of professional misconduct against key teachers were dropped. (Although the teachers were not cleared, the case against them collapsed on procedural grounds before a verdict was delivered; for reviews see Awan, 2018; Holmwood and O'Toole, 2018.[11]) Thus, the link between anti-radicalisation, anti-extremism and the requirement that schools promote British values was clear from the beginning and the Trojan Horse affair remains a shorthand for undue and subversive Muslim influence (see Chapter Five for an example). Therefore, anxiety around the behaviours and allegiances of Muslim young people and teachers have resulted in both the Prevent duty and the requirement to promote FBV in an attempt to develop an allegiance to liberal values (through the latter) and a mechanism to identify instances where this allegiance may be failing (through the former).

Reactions to FBV

After the FBV requirement was introduced, there were protests and critiques from teachers' unions, journalists and academic commentators. Key concerns were that the label 'British' was inaccurate and divisive (the values are not only subscribed to in Britain);[12] that the label may be alienating to families where parents did not consider themselves or were not formally recognised as British); that the values were imposed without discussion; that guidance was vague; and that, most importantly, as with the Prevent duty, teachers were being coopted into state securitisation processes (e.g. Richardson and Bolloten, 2014, 2015; Lander et al, 2016; Elton-Chalcraft et al, 2017; for media comment see e.g. Maylor, 2014; Rosen, 2014; Lott, 2017). Schools' immediate reaction seemed to be one of confusion (unsurprisingly). Initially, some schools were downgraded for insufficient attention to 'preparing pupils for life in modern Britain' (Long, 2018). As Vanderbeck and Johnson (2016) note, '"Preparation for later life", in this formulation, has become interpreted and expanded by Ofsted to mean a capacity to participate in a diverse, modern, liberal, democratic nation state' (p. 300). Interestingly the initial group being downgraded consisted mostly of schools with White British populations, with the criticism that little attention was being paid to student awareness of communities and beliefs different from their own (Nye, 2014). Inspector judgements have a degree of subjectivity. In an otherwise positive report, a first school (for children 5–8 years) in Worcestershire (a largely White British and rural/suburban area) was told in 2016 that 'British values have not yet been taught', which suggested that the inspectors expected explicit FBV lessons, although, as will become apparent, this is not a common response. The school in Worcestershire responded quickly, showing multiple examples of learning about British values.

Some faith schools and groups were particularly concerned with the question of whether they were expected to 'promote' same-sex relationships as part of 'preparing pupils for life in modern Britain', an issue at the intersection of faith and equality.

Sexual orientation is a protected characteristic, but same-sex relationships are often not favoured by conservative Christians, Muslims or Jews. The resolution for faith schools, where this has been a concern, appears to be one of recognising legal protection for same-sex relationships but avoiding anything that can be seen as 'promotion' or indeed approval. This stance raises questions as to whether it fully complies with the requirement to promote respect for non-heterosexual people (Vanderbeck and Johnson, 2016: 314).

Evangelical Christian, Muslim and Orthodox Jewish faith schools have been and remain a major focus for Ofsted inspections with regard to promoting FBV and preparing pupils for life in modern Britain. Indeed, the current Chief Inspector of schools, Amanda Spielman recently had to defend the service against accusations of bias against faith schooling (Spielman, 2018a). She has made several recent pronouncements about the need for a thorough promotion, indeed an 'inculcating' of British values in schools and for school leaders to demonstrate a 'muscular liberalism' in defence of liberal values against minority ethnic populations that are assumed to be challenging them (Spielman, 2017, 2018a, 2018b).

In another recent intervention, the House of Lord's committee on citizenship and civic engagement argued in favour of the FBV but suggested a more thorough citizenship education divorced from counter-extremist policy, a change in name from 'British values' – thought to be inaccurate – to the 'shared values of British citizenship', and also the replacement of 'mutual respect and tolerance' with 'respect for the inherent worth and autonomy of every person' (para 58). The government response ruled out any significant changes (MHCLG, 2018a). Indeed, there is no sign that FBV are going to disappear from the policy agenda, and the government has instructed Ofsted to 'ensure … strong coverage' of schools' promotions of FBV within its new 2019 inspection arrangements (MHCLG, 2018b: 33).

Conclusion

As policy enactment and resulting practices cannot be fully understood without knowledge of the context in which the enactment is taking place, I have focused on the features of the wider social and political environment and have introduced terminology commonly used to describe approaches to diversity. I have sought to trace both the changes in attitude signalled by the changing language and the continuity in practices, the latter forming a thin layer of past policy 'sediment' (Ball, 1994). I have also outlined specific features of the contemporary political and social context which seem to me to be relevant to understanding the formulation and enactment of the FBV policy. In brief, my argument has been that a policy mandating the promotion of liberal democratic principles has arisen from an increasing illiberal political and social landscape, one that has tilted towards xenophobia, resulting in a more pronounced stance of anxiety, defensiveness and aggression towards the 'foreigner'.

Notes

[1] Honig is writing about the US, a nation built upon and through immigration, but I think the broad outline of her theory is applicable to England because of its long-established history of immigration.

[2] See Bari 2012; Muir 2018; Katwala 2018; and Foster 2018 for examples.

[3] See e.g. ex-Labour prime minister Tony Blair's call for a 'new modern patriotism', reported in *The Guardian*, 28 March 2000, https://www.theguardian.com/uk/2000/mar/28/britishidentity.tonyblair [Accessed 9 May 2019]; the ex-Labour prime minister Gordon Brown (speaking as Chancellor of the Exchequer) in 2007 on 'a renewed focus on what it is to be British and what we value about the British way of life', https://www.theguardian.com/politics/2007/feb/27/immigrationpolicy.race [Accessed 9 May 2019]; and David Cameron (2014) on the requirement to promote British values in schools.

[4] The 'hostile environment' was apparently a name for a working group under the Coalition government that was tasked with restricting the access of undocumented migrants to benefits, employment, housing and health care. The phrase entered the public consciousness when the policy was

found to have been applied to migrants from the Caribbean – the 'Windrush generation' – who had lived in the UK for most of their lives.

5 'White privilege' is described by Peggy McIntosh as a 'package of unearned assets' based on skin colour (1992: 30).

6 For example, the replacement of the Commission for Race Equality, the Disability Rights Commission and the Equal Opportunities Commission by the Equality and Human Rights Commission in 2007.

7 'Integration' means migrants adopting practices from a majority culture without having to give up their own. 'Assimilation' describes minorities being subsumed into the majority culture.

8 The Joint Committee on Human Rights reported cautiously that 'It is too early to reach any definitive conclusions on the success of the Prevent Duty in schools. Anecdotal evidence suggests that there may be some cause for concern about the impact of the Duty' (2017: para 50).

9 Although both the National Union of Teachers and the Association of Teachers and Lecturers voiced concerns over British values and the Prevent duty, their new website (the unions have now amalgamated to form the National Education Union) includes only a brief description of the Prevent duty and FBV under the heading of 'safeguarding' (as of May 2019).

10 https://www.gov.uk/government/groups/review-of-public-sector-equality-duty-steering-group. [Accessed 9 May 2019].

11 Professional misconduct hearings were held by the disciplinary panel of the DfE's professional body, the National College for Teaching and Leadership. The panel decided in May 2017 that the hearings should not continue as a result of an abuse of process, specifically that government lawyers had withheld evidence gathered for the DfE-commissioned Clarke investigation. 'After several years and hundreds of thousands of pounds of public money, just one teacher – the former acting head of Oldknow [School] – has had any disciplinary charges upheld in relation to the Trojan horse case. The other 14 have all had their cases overturned, dropped or dismissed' (Shackle, 2017).

12 The latest policy document on counter-terrorism (Home Office, 2018d) appears to acknowledge these criticisms concerning the problematic nature of the 'British' label as on one occasion it lists the FBV, but refers to them simply as 'the values of our society' (para 303) and later describes the role of the Commission for Countering Extremism as 'promoting fundamental *pluralistic* British values' (para 306, emphasis added).

TWO

Citizenship, identity and belonging

> The general expectation that national membership comprises a commitment to a particular set of values raises new questions about people's differing commitments to these values, presenting a key resource for establishing insiders and outsiders. (Fozdar and Low, 2015: 528)

In this chapter, I argue that the policy to promote FBV is framed within a liberal version of nationalism, and consider some issues arising from this philosophy. The research data illustrate the affective aspects of citizenship, that is, in brief, the emotions that revolve around citizenship at two levels: the nation (what it is to be an adult citizen of the nation) and the school (what it is for pupils to be a current 'citizen' of a particular school). Later chapters, therefore, consider, first, whether and how the nationalist emphasis of the policy plays out in schools; second, the extent to which my research suggests that students are able to debate and discuss issues connected to national values and identity (Chapter Four); and, third, whether the mandatory promotion of FBV is a viable route for the generation of a shared national identity as seems to be the aim (Chapters Four and Six). In this chapter, I review literature on nationalism that addresses whether and how a sense of solidarity with co-nationals and commitment to a nation can be encouraged without that solidarity and commitment drawing on exclusionary understandings of who belongs.

The FBV policy is presented as an example of liberal nationalism, as it offers liberal democratic principles as the focus for citizen loyalty, as constituting what it means to be 'British'. However, I question whether commitment to this set of large-scale, abstract principles can completely erase ethnic aspects of nationalism, that is, a more tribal 'us' and 'them' identity. I continue by suggesting that the power of nationalism can be understood as emanating not simply from overt displays of national pride and identity, but also (following Billig, 1995) from its embeddedness in our everyday lives to the extent that it passes as unremarkable and taken for granted. Educating children and young people in the principles, knowledge and behaviours deemed necessary for 'good' citizenship is a commonly understood function of national education systems, and in the second half of the chapter I consider briefly some contemporary influences on citizenship education in different countries, including recent counter-extremism policies. The chapter ends with a discussion of the rise and fall of citizenship education in English schools.

Affective citizenship

I have found useful an approach to citizenship that stresses affect; that is, it focuses on bodies, feelings and emotions,[1] as discussed in the work of, for example, Fortier (2010, 2017), Di Gregorio and Merolli (2016), Johnson (2010) and Mookherjee (2005). Affective approaches understand citizenship as going beyond 'a purely rational and administrative exercise of state authority' – a series of rights and responsibilities held by rational subjects – by paying attention to how 'regimes of inclusion and exclusion' are produced (Di Gregorio and Merolli, 2016: 934).

Affective citizenship concentrates attention on citizenship as involving bodies and feelings, the nature of the emotions that attach themselves to citizenship (Fortier, 2016: 1041); it highlights how 'citizens are encouraged to feel about others and themselves' (Johnson, 2010: 496). Emotions are mobilised within the construction of citizenship, and thus 'the interaction of affect with social power relations can influence constructions of citizen identity and entitlements and involve different emotional regimes' (Johnson, 2010: 496). The idea of affective citizenship also acts to unsettle any assumptions that nations and citizens are 'monolithic constructs' (Strandbrink, 2017: 199), 'speaking with one voice' (p. 3). Affect, even if not clearly named, runs through academic discussions of citizenship, nationalism and identity. This is because these discussions explore the tensions around what holds people together, what develops a sense of communality and belonging, particularly given the movement of people between nations and the current heightened levels of popular anxiety over security, migration and integration. Healy (2018), for example, clearly signals an affective approach to citizenship when she argues that it should be understood as requiring 'belonging' across three dimensions: formal membership, a sense of belonging and a perception by others that one belongs, a formulation to which I shall return. In the next section, I briefly consider some of the core arguments in the literature on nationalism and belonging.

Citizenship and nationalism

A brief note on terminology

When I started doing this research, as a newcomer to the literature on nationalism, I quickly appreciated that the terminology used in debates is contested, so I set out here a brief explanation as to how I use some of these terms. In offering a capsule definition of nationalism, I follow Jensen and Mouritsen who cite Smith's definition of nationalism as a discourse related to 'the attainment and maintenance of autonomy, unity, and identity on behalf of a population deemed by some of its members to constitute an actual or potential "nation"' (Smith, 2000: 3, cited in Jensen and Mouritsen, 2017: 2). This definition follows the use of 'nationalism' in much of the literature but differs from its common usage as something of a latent force that explodes periodically in displays of national superiority (Ozkirimli, 2017). Instead my focus is on the sustaining of national identity.[2]

The issue of the degree of emotionality that different variants of nationalism generate remains a key issue. The FBV present a set of liberal democratic principles which appear to offer belonging to the nation to anyone who can commit to those principles. This belonging to the nation is predicated on civic rather than ethnic grounds – a long-standing, if somewhat blunt distinction in the literature on nationalism (see Kohn, 1965). Civic nationalism relies on shared commitments to political principles, whereas ethnic nationalism prioritises 'primordial, affective connections between compatriots' (Fozdar and Lowe, 2014: 524), based on shared language, heritage and ethnicity. In order to provide a shortcut through the density of scholarly literature (hopefully without presenting too many simplistic distortions), I suggest civic and ethnic nationalist emphases as positions on a continuum. At the civic end, in many readings (see e.g. Miller, 1995; Markell, 2000), would be Habermas's 'constitutional patriotism' – where abstract liberal political values, enshrined in a constitution, and not a 'concrete historical community' (Markell, 2000: 45), is the focus for loyalty and commitment. Some commentators argue that a civic nationalist state in a pure form is unlikely to exist, as its civic and nationalist elements would be in tension (Levey, 2014: 177). Thus, further along the continuum from civic nationalism lies liberal nationalism. Its proponents argue that requiring adherence to seemingly placeless principles (as in constitutional patriotism) is insufficient to achieve societal solidarity, and so a 'thicker', more emotionally engaging approach is necessary; that is, a privileging of a particular national identity is required in order to constitute the 'nation as a community of shared belief' (Miller, 1995; Soutphommasane, 2012: 72). However, this requires a precarious balance in multiethnic societies if a shared national identity is to provide a source of connection between co-nationals (Gustavasson, 2015) but not tip into ethnic nationalism where full citizenship and belonging is reserved for those sharing a particular cultural and ethnic heritage. The nature of this balance is discussed later.

A shared national identity for a diverse society?

Conversi argues that nation-building relies on the *construction* of a shared image, the power of myths, based on the assumption that 'shared identities could be fabricated from above by fostering inter-connectedness through the deliberate cultivation of common allegiances' (2014: 28). As noted earlier, the FBV policy can be understood as an exemplar of this 'deliberate cultivation' in the process of nation-sustaining (a more apt term for the British case than nation-building). As such, the policy represents a liberal nationalist approach to citizenship. Liberal nationalism asserts, for a multicultural population, a shared citizens' commitment to the society, its values and support for its institutions, rather than emphasising being born in the country and belonging to the dominant ethnic group. The national identity is promoted, not through a focus on the importance of homogeneity in private cultures and lifestyles, but through the promotion of a shared public culture through social and political institutions. This is important because 'a shared national identity' is understood as key to sustaining a liberal political community, and a 'community of shared belief' (Soutphommasane, 2012: 71) as a source of solidarity:

> [Liberal nationalism's] central contention is that the constellation of liberal political ideals – individual rights protected by the rule of law, a government administering impartial laws, a deliberative democracy, a welfare state

that redistributes resources to those in want and need – can only be achieved if there is a shared national identity among citizens motivating reciprocity and cooperation. (Soutphommasane, 2012: 71)

Similarly, Miller and Ali argue: 'When people identify with one another as compatriots, over and above the many more specific gender, ethnic, cultural or religious identities they may have, they are more likely to display generalised trust, and to show solidarity' (2014: 238; see also Banting and Kymlicka, 2017: 22). Miller's earlier work argues that a 'common public culture' is 'a set of understandings about how a group conducts its life together', noting that this understanding will include political principles and social norms (he gives the example of queuing) and may also include 'cultural ideals' (such as religious beliefs), but will leave room for different private cultures (1995: 26). Liberal nationalism is illustrated, for instance by the current 'Life in Australia' guide which includes the statement 'An important feature of Australian society today is not only the cultural diversity of its people, but the extent to which they are united by an overriding and unifying commitment to Australia' (Department of Immigration and Border Protection, 2016: 9). The use of 'overriding' here is interesting, prompting the question of whether all citizens have to override the cultural specificities of their identities to the same extent in making a commitment to Australia. The citizenship ceremony in the UK (mandatory for new citizens) includes a more general pledge to 'uphold its democratic values' (Home Office, 2013); of the values listed, most are the same as the FBV, although for unknown reasons 'mutual respect' is absent and is replaced by 'participation in community life'.

Liberal nationalism's promotion of adherence to civic rather than ethnic identities is intended to reduce the possibility of negative emotions displayed towards minorities (Miller and Ali, 2014), the focus being on shared political ideals rather than the commonality of 'blood and soil'. A recent example of this came from Ofsted's Chief Inspector when she said: 'They [the FBV] are values that give a simple message to our young people: in Britain, no matter what your background, you can fit in, you can succeed and you can belong' (Spielman, 2018b). Liberal nationalism is therefore presented as a 'safer' version of nationalism. 'The moral psychology of nationalism, with its mutually reinforcing mixture of moral conviction and communal feeling' is, as Yack (2014: 412) comments, volatile, with obvious dangers of exclusion, persecution of the 'other' and xenophobia. Yack cites Canovan's metaphor of nationalism as a battery: 'a cheap and mobile source of collective energy that can be harnessed to an extraordinary variety of causes' (Canovan, 1996: 73–4, cited in Yack, 2014: 412). Whereas nationalism based on common ethnicity is perceived as the likely generator of hostility to 'others', liberal nationalism's aim of inspiring devotion to political principles (such as democracy and rule of law) aims to keep 'the divisive force of other, more pernicious attachments at bay' (Markell, 2000: 39). The risk of this philosophy is that a focus on nationhood assumes an already existing unity and homogeneity (Kostakopoulou, 2010), and so still tends to result in individual belonging being defined in relation to an 'ethnic core' (Soutphommasane, 2012: 73). This leads to an ethnic nationalist dominance of a 'legitimate' citizen identity and the resulting exclusion of those who are not perceived to be part of the nation, who do not belong and who do not deserve to do so (Soutphommasane, 2012; Banting and Kymlicka, 2017).

However, liberal nationalists (e.g. Tamir, 1993; Miller, 1995, 2000; Soutphommasane, 2012), aware of these risks, argue that a dialogue about the meaning and constitution of nationality and national identity is fundamental, as it would allow the 'thinning' of national identity in order to accommodate religious and ethnic diversity (Banting and Kymlicka, 2017: 22) while maintaining a 'thick' enough identity to generate cohesion. Liberal nationalist writers argue for 'a dynamic national conversation through which a nation renews its self-understanding', a dialogue about 'the expression and interpretation of the community's national culture' (Soutphommasane, 2012: 76, 71). Membership of a national community implies a 'commitment to participate in a critical debate about the nature of the national culture' (Tamir 1993: 90) because a 'shared national identity is not set in aspic' (Miller, 1995: 150). 'Conversations' about national identity would be expected to result in some degree of revision of traditional ideas about (in this case) 'Britishness' in the hope of identifying and reaching areas of consensus through processes of dialogue. Exactly how these 'robust debates' (Soutphommasane, 2012: 232) would take place is not clear. Miller assumes that the process would largely be conducted through formal political institutions and that schools would simply be arenas for the reproduction of an already-agreed common national identity (1995: 142) but it would, in theory, be possible for young people in schools to contribute to such debates (for discussion, see Soutphommasane, 2012).

There are two main grounds for concern here to which I wish to draw attention. The first is the assumption that different social groups can take part in a collective debate 'on an equal footing' (Miller, 1995: 153), where all voices are heard. If this debate is to be within the formal political arena, it overlooks the social and economic barriers that may prevent people participating in, valuing or trusting a process of formal representation, and if the arena is to be (or also to be) civil society much the same objection can be made. This returns us to Healy's emphasis on three elements of citizenship: in addition to formal membership, there also has to be a sense of belonging and a perception by others that one belongs. As I discussed in Chapter One, for various minority groups one or more of these three elements may be missing, thus casting doubt on their ability to participate equally in debates on what constitutes national identity (Mason, 2018).

The second set of concerns is the likelihood of liberal nationalism successfully taming affect, namely, people's strong emotional response to nationality and identity (Markell, 2000). Unmoved by references to national conversations and critical debates (as earlier), Kostakopoulou asserts that liberal nationalism is underpinned by a conception of culture as an 'endangered species that must be defended – and not as changeable, renegotiated and reconstructed creations' (2006: 90), but rather as 'idealized' and 'oddly ahistorical' (Kostakopoulou 2006: 105). This is indeed an understanding of 'British culture' that is visible in some schools (see Chapter Four). She describes the 'fuzzy boundaries between ethnic [emphasising shared ethnicity and heritage] and civic [emphasising shared commitment to liberal political principles] understandings of nationhood' (Kostakopoulou, 2006: 73). Fozdar and Low (2015) go further and, using a broad civic/ ethnic nationalism dichotomy, discuss the ways in which, since ethno-nationalist sentiments have become socially unacceptable, objections to migrants are still expressed but in the language of civic nationalism, for example portraying minorities as illiberal in their views and as wanting to impose 'their' culture upon others (also Billig et al, 2005; Fortier, 2005). In this way,

> Civic nationalism contains a matrix of inclusion and exclusion. It may not regularly deploy stereotyped descriptions of 'our' characteristics, nor compare 'us' to a distinctly defined 'other' [as in ethnic nationalism]. However, [civic nationalism] still maintains complex systems of citizenship, which differentiate between 'us' nationals and foreigners. (Billig et al, 2005: 74; see also Closs Stephens, 2013)

Thus, although a moderate form of nationalism as endorsed by liberal nationalists does not promote overt hostility towards 'others', it still appears to have a basis of exclusive cultural identification – some groups belong and some do not.

The FBV are, on one level, a 'pure' list of civic, liberal democratic political principles without reference to ethnicity or a shared heritage, positioned at the civic end of the civic–ethnic nationalist continuum. Thus, FBV are offered as a focus for developing loyalty to the nation on the basis of it offering democracy, the rule of law, individual liberty and solidarity with others within the state through mutual respect and tolerance. However, I argue that this 'purity' is undercut by several national and local factors which emphasise a particular cultural base. National factors include the naming of the values as 'British' (a source of contention, as noted in Chapter One); the national context, shaped by politicians' pronouncements on 'Britishness', which despite nods of recognition towards a multiethnic country also draw on more exclusive representations; and recent curriculum changes in schools which emphasise 'British' history and especially literature in national exams at the age of 16. Local (school) factors include the adoption by some schools of what I call a *Representing Britain* response (see Chapter Four) which offers a particular cultural model of 'British' tastes, activities and practices.

Of course, as Müller argues, affirming a particular national identity is not 'automatically exclusionary on an ethnic basis. Events, historical figures, and broader principles themselves might well become part of a larger narrative of inclusion: *it all depends how it is done*' (Müller, 2007: 93, emphasis added). She argues for a process of integration involving both majority and minority groups (rather than minority groups assimilating into majority culture) which would, she asserts, lead to the emergence of 'a reconstituted "we"', an outcome also hoped for by those who advocate an open national 'conversation' about national identity, as described earlier. Her words, 'it all depends on how it is done', are a useful reminder of the importance of context and process, and indeed different schools respond differently to the policy imperative of promoting FBV (see Chapters Four and Five).

Banal and everyday nationalism

The possibility of developing a 'larger narrative of inclusion' (Müller, 2007: 93) appears questionable, however, when one considers the concept of 'banal nationalism'. Developed by Michael Billig (1995), this draws attention to the way in which, in established states, the idea of the nation is reproduced through everyday and mundane indicators: replication of the image of the flag; references by politicians and the media to 'we' and 'our country'; national sports teams and events; learning about national heroes; and, with regard to the UK, detailed coverage of the lives of the Royal Family. These are all unremarked, taken-for-granted instances of 'nation flagging' which permeate daily life (Billig, 1995; Koch and Paasi, 2016). Even in times unmarked by crisis, 'nationhood is near the surface of contemporary life' (Billig, 1995: 93), and is defined in particular ways.

Arguably, the mandatory promotion of a set of national values in schools is not routine and everyday, and this was indeed the basis of many critical commentaries when the policy was introduced (see Chapter One). It is, however, not clearly 'hot' nationalism (namely, overt signs of support for the state, the ultimate example being warfare) that Billig suggests is the opposite to banal nationalism.[3] Given this, I suggest the term 'everyday nationalism' (see e.g. Jones and Merriman, 2009) as a more appropriate conceptual lens through which to view FBV, as it complicates the binary divide between 'banal' and 'hot' nationalism (Antonsich and Skey, 2017). Everyday nationalism seeks to focus not just on the state's dissemination of messages about 'the nation' but also on how people take up, respond to and feel about national identity. Understanding nationalism in this way is consistent with an emphasis on understanding citizenship through a focus on affect, as it emphasises the emotional importance of a 'feeling of connection, belonging, attachment to the nation' (Militz and Schurr, 2016: 55). Such feelings are often experienced in the body, as a form of 'corporeal conviviality' (Militz and Schurr, 2016: 61); an example is the singing, chanting and waving of flags that is part of watching a national football team play. In Chapter Four, I consider the imagining of the nation by schools in their response to the British values requirement.

Moving this debate from the abstract realms of political philosophy into commentary on migration and the resulting increase in ethnic diversity in different European states (returning for a moment to the focus of Chapter One), Joppke (2010) maintains that citizenship identity is increasingly being defined by governments across Europe in universalistic terms as commitments to the principles of liberal democracy (hence, as in FBV, democracy, the rule of law and so on). However, other commentators argue that the turn of European states towards promoting 'universal' values to newcomers in fact underestimates the way in which 'these universal values and virtues are not just seen as indispensable, but as "ours" They are put at the service of defining a national "we"' (Jensen and Mouritsen, 2017: 1), a 'new form of superiority based on liberal values' (Revell and Bryan, 2018: 58–9). In this way, civic principles are redefined as a focus of ethnic nationalist sentiment (as claimed by Fozdar and Low and Billig). For example, the Danish canon, a list of Danish national values and practices created from public recommendations,[4] combines without differentiation, universal democratic principles like freedom of the individual and equality before the law, Western European traditions such as Christianity and a strong welfare state, with nation-specific traditions such as *hygge* (roughly translated as a Danish understanding of relaxation emphasising a warm atmosphere). Nationalism therefore remains an important lens through which to view these developments, despite the proliferation of appeals by European states to universal values.

A key space for the dissemination of both universal and national values is clearly the education system. In Chapters Four and Five, I explore how the case study schools respond to diversity and difference in schools. In this chapter, however, I continue by briefly indicating developments in citizenship education in a number of countries, focusing in particular on the rise and fall of citizenship education in English schools.

Directions in citizenship education

Citizenship education has traditionally focused on developing student identification with the nation. A recent collection (I. Davies et al, 2018) has focused on the take-up, constraints and possibilities of citizenship education around the world. A full discussion of these developments is beyond the scope of this book, given its specific focus on FBV. However, it is clear that despite major differences in how nations understand citizenship education – differences that are influenced by their historical, political, economic and cultural contexts – a number of common themes shape the current policy and practice of citizenship education. The first, discussed further below, is the spread of global citizenship education (GCE), reflected in the increasing number of countries incorporating an understanding of global citizenship into their policies (see e.g. Pearson et al, 2018 on Australasia and Davies et al, 2005 on England). A focus on GCE signals linkages between the local, national and global, and introduces conceptions of shared human rights that reach beyond the nation rather than emphasising membership of a particular nation-state (Osler and Starkey, 2018). This approach does not preclude national citizenship, but it does challenge exclusive understandings of it (Osler, 2011).

Additional identifiable themes and influences in approaches to citizenship education, impacting to different degrees on different countries, include globalisation and the need to maintain economic competitiveness (Sant and Gonzalez-Valencia, 2018). For example, Ho (2018) cites Sung et al's (2013) identification of some states' adoption of a stance of 'economic nationalism' with the goal of gaining advantages in global markets through having a competitive, flexible workforce together with a strong national identity. Other influences on citizenship education curricula include increased ethnic, cultural and religious diversity in many countries owing to global population flows (Banks, 2014); the high-stakes testing culture in many school systems that has led to a narrowing of the curriculum and a marginalisation of citizenship education (e.g. House of Lords Select Committee 2018 on England; Peck and Pashby, 2018 discussing the US) and the rise of character education (Peck and Pashby, 2018, discussing Canada). These latter two themes are discussed in this and later chapters in this book in relation to the English context. The last shared theme is the recent use by governments of national education systems as a medium for the promulgation of counter-extremism policies which I now briefly discuss.

Citizenship education and counter-extremism

On this last theme, L. Davies (2018), in a review of counter-extremism initiatives in education, identifies a variety of programmes in and across a range of different countries to address one or more of Islamist extremism, Islamophobia, right-wing extremism, community cohesion and intergroup conflict; to encourage criticality, conflict resolution and thinking skills (e.g. Philosophy for Children); and the further development of children's knowledge of citizen rights, democracy and citizenship (e.g. through the UNICEF Rights Respecting Schools Award[5]). Many of these initiatives are piecemeal in form, as she notes, but are likely to fall under the rather amorphous heading of citizenship/civics education. The range of issues that Davies identifies illustrates attempts by different nation-states to use the education system to address perceived tensions between unity of purpose and a diverse population.[6] Mouritsen and Jaeger (2018), in considering the role of civic education in diverse Western European societies, similarly identify an increase in interest in this topic from governments seeking a way of addressing ethnic tensions and terrorism, and a perception that community cohesion is in decline. They note considerable variations in approach as different countries pick and mix civic republicanism, communitarianism, liberal, cosmopolitan and neoliberal elements in their education programmes. In their pen portraits, they suggest, for example, that Denmark emphasises 'Danish values', while in contrast the Swedish programme presents values as dynamic and negotiable so that 'civic education became part of a post- or even anti-nationalist reaction' (Mouritsen and Jaeger, 2018: 7).

Another approach is that taken by France, which has had a long history of civic education promoting core national values through assimilation, reflecting the French Republic's tradition of universalism (van Brugel and Scholten, 2017). France has re-emphasised and further developed civic education following the 2015 terrorist attacks. Jonathan James's (2018, also James forthcoming) research presents an interesting comparison of policies aimed at preventing terrorism in France and England. Both countries understand the role of schools as promoting a liberal democratic set of values designed to lessen the possibility of extremist thought, and both encourage teachers to challenge and report ideas and behaviours that appear outside of this liberal framework (somewhat differently understood in both countries: see e.g. Werbner, 2007). However, as Wesselhoeft (2017) illustrates, in France the teacher has been traditionally and is currently understood to represent and to be responsible for the transmission of republican values, a role that has no direct parallel in England (although see Revell and Bryan's 2018 discussion of 'liquid professionalism', which they argue has broken down the boundaries between teachers and the state). James discusses '*Le grande mobilisation de l'école pour les valeurs de la République*' which includes 11 different measures and was released shortly after the January 2015 *Charlie Hebdo* terror attacks in Paris. The most widely implemented of these measures seems to be *Enseignement moral et civique* (EMC;

moral and civic education), which emphasises knowledge and understanding of republican values but also includes work on equality and anti-discrimination. EMC is a compulsory subject throughout schooling and, unlike FBV, is assessed. Together with French and mathematics, EMC has recently been described by the Ministry of Education, as 'fundamental knowledge' (James forthcoming).[7] Wesselhoeft describes 'a series of readings and debates, not only grounded in secularism and the foundational trinity of Republican values, liberty, equality, and fraternity, but also focusing on discrimination, sexism, racism, and coexistence' (2017: 633). James considers the differences between FBV and EMC and related French policies. Governments in both countries have tried to emphasise their own initiatives but practice in schools does not necessarily reflect the rhetorical status in either country. One of the most significant differences between the two countries is the key role in France of *laïcité*, a core principle of French schooling (James, 2018). *Laïcité* means, broadly, institutional secularism, thereby ensuring the separation of the state and religious organisations, and schools have been required to display a *laïcité* charter since 2013, which students and parents are expected to sign. It is a one-page document that sets out the principles of *laïcité* in accessible language. More recent documentation on the theme of *faire respecter le principe de laïcité à l'école* (e.g. Ministere de l'Education Nationale, 2018[8]) sets out guidance for school leaders which presents *laïcité* as a vehicle for the peaceful coexistence of religions and also gives guidance on how to make *laïcité* part of a positive school culture. However, James also identifies a preoccupation in policy with 'violations' of *laïcité*. Examples of possible violations include wearing a hijab (a head scarf) or contesting the theory of evolution. Violations can and should be reported to the school hierarchy, or directly to the Ministry of Education via an online portal. The French case briefly outlined here and the English Prevent duty discussed in Chapter One illustrate the extent to which governments are deploying citizenship/civics education as a mechanism by which to firmly embed schools in a securitisation agenda and to encourage 'correct' attitudes, behaviours and emotions (see Macaluso, 2016; Ragazzi, 2017; Revell and Bryan, 2018; Sukarieh and Tannock, 2018).

Citizenship education: encouraging 'correct' emotions?

As stated at the beginning of the chapter, affect clearly runs through discussions of citizenship and national and global identities, although this is not always made explicit in writing on citizenship education. An exception is provided by Hung (2010), who focuses on the processes by which citizen education directs emotions about one's own and others' loyalty and belonging, and, drawing on the work of James Banks, argues for an approach that stresses affective citizenship. Hung (2010) argues that two main approaches are in play. These repeat, with slightly different emphases, the debates outlined earlier on the tensions between unity and diversity. The first of Hung's approaches is conventional citizenship education, which he notes has been 'revitalised' as part of western anti-terrorist campaigns and seeks to equip students to accept values, knowledges and institutions as they are, and to assimilate minorities into a (presumed) majority view. Critical citizenship education, however, seeks to recognise and foster the plurality of the public sphere and to draw attention to unequal power relationships. Writers on GCE often draw a similar distinction in relation to the broad field, for example, Oxley and Morris's (2013) cosmopolitan and advocacy approach[9] and Andreotti's (2006) distinction between 'soft' and 'critical' GCE. In a systematic review of the literature, Goren and Yemini (2017) indicate the prevalence of cosmopolitan/soft/conventional approaches in classrooms (see Chapters Five and Six).

Despite this apparent avoidance of critical approaches on the ground, Hung argues that the liberal rationality underpinning a critical version of citizenship education, with its emphasis on critical thinking, would be enriched by a recognition of affect. His preferred model of affective citizenship education is a perspective that 'include[s] bodily experiences, individual idiosyncrasies, feelings, emotions and imagination as parts of citizenship' (2010: 496). Zembylas develops this position further by noting that students' feelings and emotions have not been absent from school discourses around citizenship, but agreeing that 'an integrated understanding of affective citizenship and critical citizenship [would] provide a more holistic description of the ways in which students' emotional histories are embedded in wider contexts of socio-political forces, needs and interests' (2013a: 10). Additionally, he draws attention to the 'emotional complexities and ambivalences that frequently remain unnoticed behind the use of emotional injunctions in schools' (2013a: 14):

Thinking critically about the affective aspects of citizenship may help students engage in examining the ways in which the nation-state uses various mechanisms to establish and police boundaries of belonging in the community or may help them interrogate the consequences of these mechanisms for how citizens engage in the democratic process, when students from a young age are systematically directed to feel certain emotions (e.g. pride) about the nation-state, while silencing others (e.g. shame). (Zembylas, 2015: 3)

I will return later to school events seeking to generate pride in the nation-state. Affective citizenship has been used as a way of understanding particular policy initiatives (see e.g. Fortier, 2010 and De Wilde and Duyvendak, 2016 on community cohesion policies), and I argue here that it a particularly useful focus when considering the requirement to promote British values in schools. It allows us to consider not just the requirement itself, but also how schools understand citizenship both as students as future adult citizens and as students in the present tense, as 'citizens' of their school (a frequent appellation in schools). These two foci are often overlapping, as can be seen in the rise in programmes in character, values, and moral education (variously named) which exhort students to develop particular values to guide their behaviour in school and in later life – respect, resilience and perseverance being particularly common (see Chapter Four; Suissa, 2015; Vincent, 2018). Gagen (2015) makes a pertinent comment in his analysis of social and emotional learning in schools, noting that such 'feeling' programmes are understood as advantageous to individual learning and well-being, and also 'as a fundamental constituent of citizen identity' (2015: 140) by producing emotionally literate, self-governing citizens.

The duplication between the way which the 'correct' emotional literacy is developed in school citizens and adult citizens is illustrated by the parallels between school processes and those found in a local project to increase community cohesion. De Wilde and Duyvendak's (2016) study describes the actions of local government staff in Amsterdam as they worked to generate the local population's desire for engagement with 'the community'. The researchers identify three sensitising techniques used by officials in their work with local residents: caring (informal, friendly behaviour and personal involvement with the various initiatives), appreciating (public recognition and praise of the work of residents on particular initiatives; competitions and prizes) and branding (photos and newsletters which identify the project). The techniques are, of course, very similar to the embedded, taken-for-granted ways in which teachers work in schools to try to develop a feeling of belonging and commitment to the institution among students (and staff). The aim is also the same: to develop 'particular forms of moral subjectivity' (De Wilde and Duyvendak, 2016: 989; see also Pykett et al, 2010). These ideas will be considered further in relation to the data in Chapters Four and Five. The last section of this chapter describes the contemporary policy imperatives around citizenship education in England.

Citizenship education in England

Issues of national identity and democratic values can be taught in schools in different ways, through the daily operation of the institution (e.g. through the role of students in decision making, students' relationships with adults and with peers, and how the school seeks to guide and shape those) and also explicitly (through lessons and assemblies). Citizenship education is an obvious 'home' for FBV (although leaders of the FBV training courses that I observed also suggested that schools wishing to provide Ofsted with 'evidence' should audit instances of promoting British values across the curriculum as a whole).

Since the late 1990s, citizenship education in England has risen and then fallen in prominence. A New Labour government created an advisory group which reported in 1998 (the Crick Report). Following this report,[10] statutory citizenship education was introduced in 2002 for students aged 11–16 years. Three broad overlapping strands were advocated by the Crick Report: the development of social and moral responsibility, community involvement and political literacy (Kerr, 2018). The report was criticised for, among other things, aiming to produce governable citizen subjectivities given its emphasis on neutrality (Pykett, 2007: 312), for not being sufficiently responsive to or aware of racism (Osler, 2000) and for presenting practical issues around its implementation, in terms of teacher capacity and capability, for example (McLaughlin, 2000). However, the appearance of the Crick Report certainly led to an increased legitimisation of citizenship education and many resulting initiatives in schools (Waller, 2018).

Citizenship education remains statutory in mainstream secondary schools, but this status was nearly removed in 2011 in England, and the subject was not formally reprieved until 2013. This hiatus led to a diminishing emphasis in many schools. Currently citizenship education is not statutory for fee-paying private schools, primary schools or non-maintained secondary schools (e.g. state-funded but quasi-independent schools known as academies or free schools), and is often not perceived as a high-status subject. The number of specialist-trained citizenship teachers has fallen from 243 in 2010–11 to just 54 in 2016–17, and to 40 in 2017-18.[11] Citizenship education is not necessarily taught as an independent topic in schools but is often positioned as part of PSHE (Personal, Social, Health and Economic education). PSHE covers a broad range of topics including mental health, money management, self-development, relationships with others, health and safety issues (e.g. drugs, alcohol) and careers education – a baggy holdall of topics that do not easily fit into other subjects but are understood to be important for young people to learn about (thus the list varies both over time and from school to school). If it is taught as part of PSHE, citizenship is squeezed into this long list. In secondary schools PSHE is sometimes taught in tutor time (20–30-minute daily sessions with class tutors who are usually non-specialist) and sometimes as a discrete subject (possibly taught by specialists). Given these developments, it is perhaps not surprising that the Expert Subject Advisory Group (2017) noted 'Some ambiguity about the role and status of Citizenship education', while a House of Lords report more forcefully described the government as allowing 'citizenship education in England to degrade to a parlous state' (2018: 43 para 162). The House of Lords Select Committee recommended the creation of 'a statutory entitlement to citizenship education from primary to the end of secondary education' (2018: 123, recommendation 9), a recommendation which the government has to date declined to take forward.[12]

As of March 2019 the current government programme of study for citizenship education sets out the following aim:

> Citizenship education should foster pupils' keen awareness and understanding of democracy, government and how laws are made and upheld. *Teaching should equip pupils with*

the skills and knowledge to explore political and social issues critically, to weigh evidence, debate and make reasoned arguments. It should also prepare pupils to take their place in society as responsible citizens, manage their money well and make sound financial decisions. (DfE 2013 Programme of study, emphasis added)

I shall discuss the extent to which pupils do have the opportunity to 'explore political and social issues critically' in Chapter Five. There has also been debate as to how far the Prevent duty (see Chapter One) may incur upon the exploration of social and political issues, although the Prevent Guidance to schools (Home Office, 2015) states that the duty is not intended to stop pupils debating controversial issues but rather to give them the safe space of the classroom in which to do so (Home Office, 2015: 5). The Association of Citizenship Teachers note that there is some tension here between 'facilitating the discussion of controversial issues (which implies there are a variety of valid viewpoints) and the need to challenge some views or even report them to senior colleagues (which implies some views are forbidden)' (Expert Subject Advisory Group for Citizenship 2015: 2; see also O'Donnell 2016, 2017; Bryan, 2017). The risk is that this situation may lead to what O'Donnell calls 'pedagogical injustice' because the lack of clarity over definitions and manifestations of extremism and radicalisation means that 'neither teacher nor student can fully know which ideas, views, interpretations and thoughts are permissible' (O'Donnell, 2017: 179). She argues that Muslim students are particularly affected, 'and withdrawing from discussion of controversial issues or avoiding speaking their mind. They cannot trust their teachers to be virtuous hearers, sensitive to context and willing to make singular judgements if those same teachers are also being asked to report back on indicators of risk and if their schools are being inspected on such' (2017: 180; see also Chapter Five; Sukarieh and Tannock,

2016; Thomas, 2016; Miah, 2017; Ragazzi, 2017; Revell and Bryan, 2018; Saeed, 2018).

This analysis of the English case leaves us with a picture of a constrained and narrow citizenship curriculum. However, what is taught in classrooms, how it is taught and what is contained in a policy document may not always clearly match up, especially when the guidance is loose and open, as in the case of FBV, and offers teachers the potential space and freedom to devise their own programme. This is further explored in the next chapter.

Conclusion

This chapter has discussed the importance of understanding citizenship not simply as a legal status and a series of rights and obligations, but as being shot through with affect: how people feel about citizenship, and their own and other people's claims to that position.

My starting point in this chapter was that FBV presents a list of liberal political and social principles in a way that offers belonging to the nation to anyone who commits themselves to the maintenance of these principles. There is, then, 'an un-interrogated assumption that anybody, in so far as they "enter into the bargain of intelligibility" (Berlant, 2001: 49–50) – that is, to put it simply, that they speak the right language and do the right thing – has unproblematic access to citizenship and legal/legitimate personhood' (Fortier, 2008: 33). However, the earlier discussion interrogates that assumption, noting arguments that 'pure' civic nationalist principles may be difficult to operationalise into a 'hearts and minds' commitment, as they lack emotional weight. Given that conclusion, liberal rather than 'pure' civic nationalist regimes seem almost inevitable. (As a reminder, liberal nationalist regimes promote commitment to liberal democratic principles but also emphasise a concern with developing a shared culture to which people are emotionally attached). Yet, as discussed earlier, there is some scepticism over the likelihood of political grounds for belonging (e.g. commitment to political principles) being asserted over cultural ones (e.g. shared cultural understandings, shared background) and scepticism about the vision of some liberal nationalists of an empowering and dynamic national conversation which avoids privileging particular voices. Antonsich makes a similar point, 'that the majority group's claim of the public sphere as culturally and ethnically neutral is a stratagem for delegitimising the cultural-ethnic claims of minorities. In sum, the civic, liberal national space hides a particularistic cultural definition of who can be a "proper" citizen' (Antonsich, 2016: 1793).

If we lay aside scepticism for the moment, it is possible to imagine that the promotion of FBV in schools may form part of a 'national cultural dialogue' about national identity (Soutphommasane, 2012: 12), although finding appropriate spaces within the school curriculum is challenging as one possibility, citizenship education, has become a marginalised subject in many English schools. Additionally, there are concerns both in England and elsewhere that current counter-extremist agendas may be preventing rather than encouraging pluralist understandings and critical thinking (Sukarieh and Tannock, 2016; Novelli, 2017; O'Donnell, 2017). Nonetheless, I explore this proposition further in Chapters Four and Five, focusing on the degree to which 'ethno-cultural membership, citizenship and identification with the state' are bound together (Goode, 2018: 275). A study of teachers' understandings and promotions of FBV can help shed light on this relationship.

Notes

[1] For the purposes of this book, I am unconvinced of the need to distinguish between affect and emotion, following Zembylas (2016a), Ahmed (2014) and Fortier who argues that: 'Rather, I conceive of affect and emotions as irreducibly entangled; as Sara Ahmed puts it (2014, 208), "[e]motions ... involve bodily processes of affecting and being affected". Following on

from that, I use the term affect to designate a generic category of emotions and feelings, including embodied and sensory feelings through which we experience the world, and through which worlds, subjects and objects are enacted and brought forth' (2016: 1039). For a more extended discussion see e.g. Wetherell, 2014.

2   'Nationalism' and 'patriotism' are often used interchangeably in general conversation. Goode (2018), in discussing the differences, notes that for some commentators 'patriotism and nationalism are overlapping and flexible political languages'. For others, patriotism is a positive emotion of pride in the country and nationalism is an assertion of superiority, an intolerance of 'others'. Goode argues, however, from his case study of Russia that patriotism need not be treated as distinct from nationalism (2018: 276; see also Strandbrink, 2017).

3   Billig did later acknowledge that banal and hot nationalism exist on a continuum rather than being either/or alternatives (Antonsich and Skey, 2017).

4   'The purpose of the canon is to 'prepare the ground for better integration – including of non-ethnic Danish citizens' [...] and clarify what creates Danish 'national identity and cohesion, to give us all a better sense of self and general education, create solidarity and make us a people of increased cultural awareness and common cultural experience' https://www.danmarkskanon.dk.

5   Philosophy for Children is a programme designed to promote the skills of dialogue and debate. The Rights Respecting School Award recognises schools that put children's rights – based on the UN Convention on the Rights of the Child – at the heart of their organisation.

6   It is important to note that diversity is commonly understood as ethnic, religious and/or cultural rather than economic.

7   EMC is examined in the vocational baccalaureate, and is part of the coursework element in the recently relaunched academic baccalaureate. I am very grateful to Jonathan James for providing me with up-to-date information on the French situation.

8   For an explanation of the principles of *laïcité*, and the schools' charter, see https://www.education.gouv.fr/cid95865/la-laicite-a-l-ecole.html [Accessed 9 May 2019]. It is interesting to note that one policy measure includes a *conseil des sages* (literally, council of sages) composed of academics to develop a common doctrine and understanding of *laïcité*. This doctrine is 'translated' into practical application by a national *l'équipe nationale laïcité et fait religieux* (National Laïcité and Religious Facts Team) and 30 local 'teams' (*équipes académiques laïcité et fait religieux*, local authority *laïcité* and religious facts team), with one role being to providing consistency across

the country in relation to perceived 'violations' of *laïcité*. Again, I am very grateful to Jonathan James for this information.

9   Oxley and Morris's (2013) conception of GCE as involving two broad approaches: cosmopolitan (divided into political, moral, economic and cultural categories, but with an underlying conception of universalist, hegemonic accounts of global citizenship) and advocacy approaches (social, environmental, spiritual and critical approaches, with the latter in particular exploring 'a politics of social transformation' [Dei, 2008: 479, cited in Oxley and Morris, 2013: 313]).

10 Prior to this, citizenship had been a cross-curricular theme rather than a discrete subject in the National Curriculum.

11 https://www.parliament.uk/business/publications/written-questions-answers-statements/written-question/Commons/2017-01-30/62229/ [Accessed 9 May 2019]. Also HoL, 2018 p. 35 para 127.

12 However the 2019 inspection framework (Ofsted 2019) places slightly more emphasis on pupils' 'personal development' which includes citizenship education.

THREE

Researching the promotion of fundamental British values in schools

There is much more to the research process than ever gets into the pages of articles and books. Our work has been full of loose ends, omissions and false trails. It has been punctuated by buts and maybes, by avoidance and considerable perplexity ... We have not always managed to write what it was we were trying to think. (Ball et al, 2012: 17)

Policy enactment

In this chapter, I discuss the processes of policy enactment 'policy as text' and 'policy as discourse', adding that it is also important to consider the affective policy 'tone'. I identify some key characteristics of the current English educational context, and then move on to the research design, introducing the schools and the teachers and noting some limitations to the research (also indicated by the opening quotation).

I start by outlining my understanding of the relationship between policy and practice. Policy sociology is an approach to policy analysis that emphasises, first, the importance of context in order to understand the enactment of any policy and, second, that there is no simple straight line between what a policy text states and what happens on the ground (Ball, 1994; see also S. Taylor et al, 1997; Rizvi and Lingard, 2009), hence the term 'enactment' rather than 'implementation' (Ball et al, 2012). Enactment describes the processes by which those who operate at ground level, teachers and other state-employed officials – Lipsky's (1983) 'street level bureaucrats' – interpret and reinterpret policy, translating it to fit their own contexts. They do this in terms of both what they understand to be the needs of their students or clients and their understanding of what can mentally, physically and emotionally be achieved. However, this does not mean that the space for interpretation and translation[1] is endless; rather, it is constrained by what seems to be possible to do and think – the limits of discourse. In their study of enactment, Ball et al remind us that 'Policies [act] as discursive strategies; for example sets of texts, events, artefacts and practices that speak to wider social processes of schooling, such as the production of "the student", the "purposes of schooling" and the construction of "the teacher"' (2012: 16).

In his earlier work, Stephen Ball (1994) has made an often cited distinction between policy as text and policy as discourse. Policy as text emphasises, in addition to the broader social context, the micro-politics of the particular local context, both among those who write the text and those who 'translate' it into practice. This includes the history, relationships and values and beliefs of both those groups and the wider circles of influence upon them. For instance, schools may respond to policy initiatives in very different ways depending on their current Ofsted rating or the perceived 'needs' of their local populations; the role of particular teachers, and mid-level 'policy enactors' (Singh et al 2013; e.g. trainers offering sessions on how to 'do' British values), can be key in terms of outcome; the pressure of work may affect all actors involved (Braun et al, 2011). The role of ad hocery – making do, improvisation – cannot be overlooked (Ball, 1997). Policy texts do not derive from or enter institutional vacuums – these contexts are all peopled with individuals who have their own histories and values and who change over time (Ball, 1993; Braun et al, 2010). Each new policy competes for space and attention, and may react in different ways in concert with existing policies. There are also layers of policy 'sediment' (Ball, 1994), the remaining grains of previous initiatives that act to shape the direction new ones take, as with the example of schools promoting 'community cohesion' in Chapter One. My data shows that, although the language of 'community cohesion' may have disappeared in schools, some traces of these and indeed older 'multicultural' policies still exist in an amorphous set of commitments vaguely expressed as providing a harmonious school 'community' where the students feel they belong and are treated equally, and that this is still a powerful motivator of practice (discussed further in Chapter Five).

Policy demands vary in their explicitness and force. In their study, Ball et al (2012) contrast 'personalised learning' with policy setting targets for schools, which command much teacher time and attention. Personalised learning, they argue, was largely absorbed by schools who saw it as a key part of what they did anyway, a response that has parallels with the enactment of the British values policy as described in Chapters Four and Five. The British values policy text is indeed a loose, enabling one – the guidance (DfE, 2014) has only seven pages of text. It asserts that the promotion of FBVs is part of the existing statutory duty held by maintained schools[2] 'to promote the spiritual, moral, social and cultural (SMSC) development of their students' (Education Act, 2002, section 78). The understanding and knowledge expected of students as a result of schools promoting FBV is listed as including an understanding of democratic decision making; an appreciation of religious freedom and the protection offered by the rule of law; an acceptance of the beliefs of others; and an understanding of the importance of combatting discrimination.

Examples of possible activities are given that may help students understand a range of faiths and also the practice of democracy (e.g. school councils and mock elections). So the policy text is non-specific: it allows teachers to respond with creativity, to make sense of the policy on their own, to interpret and translate, and to develop their own resources or use those developed by others (a mini-boom in commercially produced FBV resources is evident). An in-depth response to the policy, however, would require that teachers have the time and inclination to plan one, and some of the responses visible in schools – putting up posters listing the FBV, for example – were clearly (rational) exercises in making a mandated response as quickly and as easily as possible, given the intensity of teachers' workloads.

Teachers' capacity for interpretation and translation is not endless, however, and this is where Ball's Foucauldian understanding of policy as discourse comes in. 'There are real policy struggles over the interpretation and enactment of policies. But these are set within a moving discursive frame which articulates and constrains the possibilities and probabilities of interpretation and enactment' (Ball, 1994: 23). There are two sets of discourses discussed in this book. One is the dominant understanding of a 'good' teacher in a neoliberal education climate discussed in Chapter Five. The other, as I argued in Chapter One, is the broader set of discourses around 'foreigners', increasingly discourses of anxiety and suspicion about people who may not behave 'like us', do what 'we' do or believe in what 'we' believe. The immigrant, the (assumed to be conservative) Muslim and those who are understood as being resistant to integration are positioned as an obstacle to cohesion. For cohesion is the desired state where people come together and differences are forgotten; it is often claimed to appear momentarily and tantalisingly at Royal celebrations and at sporting tournaments. However, as argued earlier, alongside this and entangled in it in complex ways are different impulses: an impulse to welcome difference, to see ourselves as tolerant, convivial and cosmopolitan (Closs Stephen,

2013). Identifying this ambiguity around diversity, Closs Stephens notes that 'cultural difference' is often presented variously as 'something to be both feared and celebrated' (2013: 65). I suggest therefore that, in addition to policy as text and policy as discourse, we need to focus attention on these affective elements of the policy enactment process in relation to both teacher subjectivity (Chapter Five) and the affective[3] characteristics of the wider social and political climate. It is to this that I now turn.

Ben Anderson's (2016) definition of 'affect' as 'an umbrella category' is useful here to describe 'distinct ways of organizing the "feeling of existence"' (2016: 735). Anderson argues that we need to pay attention to the affective properties of a particular time period in a particular place, what he calls a geo-historical nexus, and to consider 'the ways in which collective affects form part of the conditions through which economic–political formations come to form and are lived' (Anderson, 2016: 739).

Anderson takes Raymond Williams's well-known term 'structure of feeling' and the more current term 'atmospheres' (2016: 736) as two ways of understanding affect in relation to contemporary political and social formations. He cites Williams's definition of 'structures of feeling' (1961/2011: 63) as the 'felt sense of the quality of life' in a defined period (Williams, 1977: 132, cited in Anderson, 2016: 745–6). Williams defines structures of feeling as a way of analysing social change that insists on the affective, everyday life experience but also maintains a focus on mediating structures; thus the term refers to the affective, bodily, emotional experience of living in a particular period of time: 'it is as firm and definite as "structure" suggests, yet it operates in the most delicate and least tangible parts of our activity' (Williams, 1961/2011: 65). Zembylas observes:

Williams insists on the emotional aspect. 'Feeling' exists within a framework, or structure, articulated as social *and* personal, the result of intersubjective *and* political relations and processes … Structures of feeling name the simultaneous cultural and discursive dimension of our experience but do not neglect that these experiences are also felt and embodied ... The notion of 'structures of feeling' describes the ways in which ideologies reflect emotional investments that remain unexamined during our daily interactions, because they have been woven into what is considered common sense. (Zembylas, 2002: 193–4)

Anderson notes that structures of feeling are 'dispersed moods' (2016: 746) that extend beyond particular sites. I have earlier described a contemporary structure of feeling in terms of an uneven balance between xenophobia and xenophilia. His second understanding of affect is in terms of affective atmospheres: 'Atmospheres are ephemeral affective impressions that envelope particular enclosed forms' (2016: 746) such as a meeting or, I suggest, a classroom. He talks also of policy 'tone' resulting from a 'cluster of more or less vague affective impressions [that] accompany a policy' (2016: 744).

In discussing school responses to FBV in the next two chapters, I want to keep these ideas in mind and to explore the tone of the policy ensemble of securitisation, and the atmosphere that the policy ensemble, and particularly the requirement to promote FBV, both responds to and provokes. First, I want to identify key characteristics of the current education policy context, after which I shall go on to introduce the schools involved in the research.

The educational context

The contemporary English educational context is defined by an established neoliberal emphasis on competition, external accountability, a diversification of educational providers and the imperative of ensuring global economic competitiveness (Ball, 2017). The pace of life in schools is one of 'hyperactivity' (Dunleavy, 1987), as changing curricula and forms of assessment are introduced. Testing is high stakes for schools as the results of national tests for students at 11, 16 and 18 years are published and are used by parents in making their choice of school and by Ofsted inspectors in making their judgements. This leads to an evaluation regime through what one headteacher in this research called a "military language" of "targets and delivery". Added to these factors are the broader circumstances affecting all state schools, of concerns with school funding and teacher recruitment and retention (DfE, 2018a; Adams, 2018).

When visiting schools, I asked teachers to direct me to those sessions where they felt that British values were being promoted. This led me to observe an eclectic range of activities – from primary school pupils' videos about good manners to lessons with secondary students about terrorism and the Holocaust, via a coffee morning held by students for senior citizens and several student council meetings. Relatively few of these events included an explicit discussion of British values. Indeed, much advice on promoting FBV recommends embedding the promotion of the values into the operation of the school and across the curriculum. However, religious education (RE), PSHE and citizenship education were identified by respondents as particularly appropriate contexts for the promotion of FBV. The low status of citizenship education is discussed in Chapter Two. Additionally, PSHE is not statutory in its entirety (health education will be by 2020), and its content varies between schools. RE must be taught by all state-funded schools in England (although parents can choose to withdraw their children from it), but it is not part of the National Curriculum and low standards and weak teaching have been identified by Ofsted (see Long, 2016). Moreover, the government encourages secondary schools to focus on a range of traditional academic subjects, a combination known as the English Baccalaureate (EBacc).[4] Citizenship education, RE and PSHE are not included in the EBacc, which led to a diminution in their status. The EBacc is part of a suite of policy reforms brought in by Michael Gove (Secretary of State for Education, 2010–14), which emphasised a more traditional subject-centred curriculum, with a focus on British literature and history. Sally Tomlinson (2019) cites a 2013 speech of Gove's in which he said that his reforms were intended to encourage the 'cultivation of the habits of proper thought', reflecting a shift in what was considered and validated as 'proper' knowledge and what was not. There has also been a rise in interest in character or values education, (further discussed in Chapter Four) which, I shall argue, has contributed to a particular – and narrowing – understanding of the personal development of young people. Having highlighted some of the key elements shaping the current educational policy context in English schools, I shall now outline the process of collecting the data and introduce the schools.

The respondent school and teachers

This book draws on an empirical data set of 56 interviews and 49 observations. The majority of these (38 interviews and 45 observations) are from nine case study schools (four primary and five secondary) with different student demographics. These nine schools are mostly within Greater London but include three in other parts of the country – the North-East, the South-West and the Midlands. I offer pen portraits of them here. They are all state-funded schools and include academies and local–authority-maintained schools,[5] with one being a faith school. They serve a wide variety of student populations in terms of both ethnicity and social class. In addition, I conducted one-off interviews with senior leaders at eight schools, including two faith schools, which allowed me to reach a wider range of schools. I also spoke with 10 other individuals who have a professional interest in the British values policy (e.g. faith school advisers, those offering training in SMSC and FBV and teacher union representatives). These data are not much discussed here because of limitations of space, but they contribute to this analysis. Finally, I also attended four training sessions/conferences on the teaching of British values. The data was hand coded, drawing on initial theoretical categories in existing literature on cohesion, citizenship and policy enactment. These codes were then refined and challenged through further engagement with and scrutiny of the data. For example, the growing emphasis in schools on values/character education emerged from the data and has proved an important element in the analysis.

Identifying and negotiating access to schools for this research presented a number of challenges. First of all, all English schools are required to promote FBV, so there was the question of where to start. My main criterion was that the eight case study schools I initially envisaged (I ended up with nine) would cover between them a range of student populations in terms of ethnicity and social class. I knew that project-funding constraints would mean that most of the schools needed to come from the Greater London area. Racial, religious and/or linguistic diversity is growing in schools outside major urban centres, but these levels of diversity are much higher in London than elsewhere in the country. The three case study schools which were outside London had predominantly White British populations.

I started by contacting a number of schools based on comments about their promotion of FBV in recent inspection reports. However, cold calling did not lead to access. In most of the case study schools, I had an indirect contact with a senior leader through someone who was more familiar to them. One primary school was recruited through my meeting with a teacher on a training course. Along the way, I came across other people who were willing to talk to me but who did not want the school to be a case study, so, as noted earlier, I included a further eight schools where I conducted a one-off interview with a teacher or senior leader. The case study schools cover a range of social and ethnic populations, the one-visit schools include four which have high numbers of Muslim students, a valid emphasis given the policy focus on Muslims (of course not all these students can be assumed to be practising Muslims or to form a homogeneous population). Workload was usually given as a reason why access was rejected, and this is unsurprising given the serious concerns around workload in the profession (DfE, 2018a). The inclusion of observations probably did not make access easier. Even experienced teachers displayed some unease about me being in the classroom, despite my repeated attempts at reassurance. This unease was rarely spoken, but displayed itself through bodies held tensely, lack of eye contact with me and occasional later comments that revealed that lesson planning had been more elaborate than usual. However, in interview teachers were far more relaxed and forthcoming.

All research has limitations, and this research, which explores the promotion of FBV in a small sample of schools, is clearly no exception. I cannot make any claims for the findings of the research beyond the context of those schools that participated in the study. The data also present a snapshot of the practices in the schools at the time when I visited, as filtered through the impressions of the particular respondents. Schools have a momentum of their own – the days are crowded and eventful, and it was impossible as a researcher to control the flow of the school day, so sometimes lessons or people I was expecting to see did not happen or were not available. There was much to commend and admire in the schools that I have not space to comment on here. Teachers are presented with an impossible task (discussed further in Chapter Five) conducted in contexts that are financially restricted and driven from outside the profession by managerial accountability measures. The promotion of FBV was another task imposed on them without consultation or indeed much guidance. Yet, despite the fact that they are routinely asked to solve societal problems that are broader than education and are working under great pressure, the teacher-respondents were uniformly helpful, interested in and thoughtful about the promotion of national values.

Next, I present a penportrait of the nine case study schools and brief details of the eight schools I visited once. I have indicated in their pseudonyms where the schools have academy status (of the case study schools, Downs and Moreton Grange were academies when I visited, Holy Church became an academy after my initial visits and Kenton became an academy after the fieldwork period). Where not indicated as an academy, the schools are maintained by the local authority. I cannot comment on the effects of academy status on the schools' promotion of FBV, as the schools had very different trajectories to becoming academies; they all belong to different small, local chains and are differently positioned in local markets. Neither have I commented on the effect of Holy Church's faith-based status on the enactment of FBV. The school was perhaps unusual, as the diocese appeared to have a limited role in the school's operation during the fieldwork period, and the teachers had a considerable degree of autonomy.

In order to avoid compromising the anonymity of the schools or any particular individuals, I have avoided giving some precise details. However, I have indicated the ethnic mix of the school's population and also whether the number of students who are or have been eligible for free school meals in the last six years is below or above the national average (this measure is known as 'FSM ever', and is a rough proxy indicator of poverty). In addition, in later chapters, I have also used teachers' descriptions of the school population to determine broad social class descriptions. All the case study schools are coeducational except for Holy Church. To help the reader keep track of the case study schools, I have also indicated one feature about their practice that is particularly relevant to FBV.

Case study schools

Garden Primary School

Garden is a large, popular and expanding primary school on a quiet suburban road. The school has over 700 pupils and a majority British South Asian population with a smaller population of children from Eastern European backgrounds. The school is an Ofsted-rated 'outstanding' school with above-average results in English and maths when children leave at the age of 11 (2016–17). The 2016–17 'FSM ever' figure was lower than the national average for primary schools which is 24.9 per cent. The school has a strong strand of work around identity and equalities.

Southern Primary School

Southern is a popular primary school serving a large urban housing estate which is currently being redeveloped, but has had a difficult history in terms of disadvantage and decline. The school serves over 450 pupils. It is a recently inspected and Ofsted-rated 'outstanding' school, with above-average results when children leave at 11 years (2016–17). Over 90 per cent of the children come from minority ethnic backgrounds, with those of Black African heritage forming the largest group. The 'FSM ever' figure is considerably above the national average of 24.9 per cent. The school is strongly values led and staff explicitly teach and assess the children on a range of values.

Newton Primary School

Newton is a very large, popular primary school of over 900 pupils, located close to a town centre in a highly deprived area. The school was recently inspected by Ofsted, and rated 'good'. The percentage of pupils who achieve the expected standards at 11 years is just above the local authority and national averages (2016–17). Over 90 per cent of the school's population come from minority ethnic backgrounds, with British Asian heritage and British Black African-heritage children forming the largest groups. The 'FSM ever' figure is slightly over the national average of 24.9 per cent. The school uses Philosophy for Children, a scheme intended to teach children how to create and then debate their own philosophical questions.

Shire Primary School

Shire is situated in a suburban area, just outside a mid-sized city. The school building is set in large and attractive grounds and houses 400 pupils. The school was deemed by Ofsted to 'require improvement' in 2014, but after the appointment of a new headteacher the next inspection judged the school to be 'good'. Results for pupils leaving at 11 years in 2016–17 were around the national average. The vast majority of the pupils are from White British backgrounds and the area surrounding the school contains affluent as well as less affluent residents. The school has a less deprived population than either Newton or Southern and the 'FSM ever' rate for the school is under the national average of 24.9 per cent. The school uses Jigsaw, a commercially available scheme that claims to offer a comprehensive approach to PSHE teaching, including the promotion of FBV.

Downs Secondary Academy

Downs is a well-established, large and very popular secondary school for 11–19-year-olds in a small town in an otherwise rural area. The school is part of a small Multi-Academy Trust (MAT), and recruits from a wide catchment area given the rural/suburban nature of its surroundings and its positive local reputation. In 2017 the Progress 8 score was average, and the Attainment 8 score was just above local authority and national averages.[6] The school is rated by Ofsted as 'outstanding'. The pupils are largely from a White British background. The 'FSM ever' figure is considerably below the national average (for secondary school populations) of 29.1 per cent. The school has established expertise in teaching about the Holocaust.

Kenton Secondary School

Kenton is a large 11–16-years secondary school in a highly deprived urban area. It has an attractive building with considerable grounds. Due to a dip in exam results, the school was judged to 'require improvement' in 2016. After the fieldwork period, the school became an academy in a small local MAT. The 2016–17 'FSM ever' percentage was over 70 per cent, the highest of all the case study schools in this research. The student population is very diverse in terms of ethnicity, the main groups being British Black African, British Bangladeshi and White British/Other. The school has strong religious education teaching.

Holy Church Secondary School

Holy Church was a small Catholic girls' school which was undersubscribed due to falling rolls, as single sex and Catholic education became less popular in the locality. It became an academy in a small regional chain just after the initial fieldwork visits. The school is located in one of the more deprived areas of an urban locality often assumed to be affluent. The 'FSM ever' percentage is much higher than the national average of 29.1 per cent. The school has a highly diverse multiethnic population, with girls of British Black Caribbean and Black African heritage making up over a third of the population. The school has strong teaching in PSHE.

Moreton Grange Secondary Academy

Moreton Grange is a well-established, popular 11–19-years school in a deprived locality within a somewhat isolated town. It is part of a small local MAT. Its last inspection rated it 'good'. The Progress 8 and Attainment 8 score for 2016–17 were above the local and national averages. The student population is overwhelmingly White British, and the 'FSM ever' percentage is well over the national average of 29.1 per cent. The school focuses on raising student aspirations.

Valley High Secondary School

Valley High is a large 11–18-years comprehensive school in an affluent urban locality. It has a highly diverse student population in terms of ethnicity, although the number of local White British middle-class children the school recruits is growing. The 'FSM ever' percentage remains above the national average. The school is judged by Ofsted to be 'good'. In 2017 the Progress 8 measure was above average, and the Attainment 8 score over the local authority and national averages. The school has an emphasis on student voice.

Other schools involved in the research

The names of these schools appear in the text in *italics* as a reminder to the reader that these schools were ones where only one interview with a senior leader took place.

Albernay Secondary School

This school is girls only, with a majority working-class population of British Asian Muslim heritage.

East Heath Secondary School

This is a boys-only school, relatively close to Albernay, with a majority working-class population of British Asian Muslim heritage.

Beit se-fer Primary

Beit se-fer, an Orthodox Jewish state-funded school, is a boys-only primary school with largely middle-class population

Talib School

A Muslim state-funded primary school, Talib is a coeducational primary school with a largely working-class population.

Point High Academy

Located in an affluent area, this secondary academy is coeducational and has a diverse population in terms of social class and ethnicity.

Marina Grammar School

This selective school is boys only and has a largely middle-class population. Entry is based on results in English and maths exams taken by 10–11-years-olds.

Millnort Secondary School

This school has a working-class coeducational population, largely of British Asian heritage.

Union Primary Academy

This academy is part of a MAT. It is a coeducational, with a working-class population. The children are from diverse ethnicities, with a significant (nearly 40 per cent) White British population.

The teachers

My contact in each case study school directed me towards teachers they thought were most involved in enacting the FBV policy in each school. I spoke to between two (Holy Church) and six (Downs, Garden) teachers at each of the case study schools and conducted between seven (Garden) and four (Holy Church, Shire) observations. Over two thirds of the school respondents were White British, with the rest being of British Black African/Caribbean or British Asian heritage. Two could be classified as White Other. The majority of the teachers I spoke to were female, particularly in the primary schools.

There is limited space to discuss particular individuals in the analysis presented here, although different ethnicities, religions, histories, career trajectories and school experiences are clearly important in determining individual responses to FBV. For example, other analyses have argued that those teachers who have minority ethnic backgrounds may be more critical of the FBV policy than some of their White British counterparts (eg Busher et al, 2017; Panjwani, 2016), but more analytical work remains to be done in the future. However, I argue here that one of the important findings of this account is the remarkably consistent views of the teacher–respondents regarding the British values policy and their role as teachers in promoting liberal values.

Conclusion

I have outlined here the broad understanding of policy enactment that I am using and, drawing on the discussion in Chapter One, I have identified the importance of the affective tone of policy as influencing enactment. I have also described the research design and participating schools and teachers. Next, I turn to the different responses made to the FBV requirement.

Notes

[1]   Ball et al distinguish between 'interpretation' – an initial, making sense of policy – and 'translation' the process of creating institutional texts and putting them into practice (2012: 43-45). 'Interpretation is about strategy and translation about tactics' (2012: 47).

[2]   Maintained state schools are those run ('maintained') by local authorities. Other state funded schools are the quasi-independent academies and free schools.

[3]   As in Chapter 2, I am using 'affect' as 'principally elided with the concept of emotion where emotions are understood as profoundly social' (Maxwell and Aggleton, 2013: 5).

4   The EBacc subjects are English language and literature, maths, the sciences (including computer sciences), geography or history, and a language.

5   As noted above, maintained schools are those that are 'maintained' (overseen) by the local authority. Academies are state-funded schools run independently of local authority (local state) control. Many are now organised into MATs (Multi-Academy Trusts). They do not have to teach the National Curriculum but are subject to Ofsted inspections.

6   Progress 8 and Attainment 8 scores indicate exam performance at the age of 16. Progress 8 measures pupil progress through secondary education in eight subjects. Attainment 8 measures pupil achievement across eight subjects. The score for each secondary school is publicly available.

FOUR

Promoting British values in schools

> Derby Day, Henley Regatta, Cowes, the twelfth of August, a cup final, the dog races, the pin table, the dart board, Wensleydale cheese, boiled cabbage cut into sections, beetroot in vinegar, nineteenth century Gothic churches and the music of Elgar. (TS Eliot, 1948: 31, describing English culture)

As noted in the last chapter, the FBV requirement is expressed in a generally worded policy text. The values themselves – democracy, the rule of law, individual liberty, mutual respect and tolerance – are examples of what Edelman (1964) called 'condensation symbols', concepts that invoke positive emotional reactions while remaining broadly defined in order to generate as much consensus as possible. This abstract emotionality precludes recognition of these values as subject to differing interpretations. Unsurprisingly all the teacher–respondents voiced support for these values (see also Janmaat, 2018 on young people's support for the FBV). Indeed, to speak against them is evidence of 'extremist' belief according to the 2015 Prevent duty guidance (Home Office, 2015: 2). The only value that generated any criticism was tolerance, with a minority of respondents noting that tolerance is a limited emotion, 'an intermediate between whole-hearted acceptance and unrestrained opposition' (Scanlon, 2003: 187) and is dependent on the generosity of those doing the tolerating. This limitation is especially clear when 'tolerance' is uncoupled from 'mutual respect', as in local versions of the FBV policy (from some schools and advisory organisations), which identify five rather than four separate values. Additionally, inherent in the concept of toleration is the power *not* to tolerate (e.g. Horton, 1996: 28; Bowie, 2018). As one teacher said, " 'Tolerance' has really negative connotation of 'we will put up with you'" (Rose, Valley High, urban area, mixed class, multiethnic population).

A key characteristic of the generally worded policy text has been the limited guidance on how to enact promotion of the FBV. Therefore, schools have responded differently, although there are observable patterns. Here, and in Chapter Five, I have identified four main approaches: *Representing Britain*, *Repackaging the FBV*, *Relocating the FBV* and *Engagement with the FBV* (the latter is discussed in Chapter Five). These are not entirely discrete, however, and some of the case study schools drew on a mixture of responses.

Representing Britain

The first approach — *Representing Britain* — was not the predominant approach taken by the case study schools in my research, but it remains very visible in FBV commercially produced resources and on school websites, and has been described in other research (e.g. Sant and Hanley, 2018; Moncrieffe and Moncreiffe, 2019). I suggest that *Representing Britain* has two elements. One is the minimalist approach of posters and displays listing FBV, often with Union-Jack-themed decoration. Some individual schools have added (often without differentiation) other values: responsibility, good manners, contributing to the community, sharing and equality are all relatively common examples. Given the 'hyperactivity'

(Dunleavy, 1987) of the policy climate, this can be understood as a rational time-saving response, producing something tangible that can be displayed to Ofsted (Ball et al, 2012). One headteacher in my research, who had been involved in a public critique of the FBV policy, described a colleague's response:

> 'I spoke to one headteacher and he said, "I don't know why you are fussing about this …", he said, "we have laminated all the key words from the British Values document, put them up round the corridors and we are done"… Because it just got it out of his way, you know.' (Elliott, *Marina Grammar*, academically selective, boys' school)

Similarly, the headteacher at Downs Academy told me that nothing additional had been necessary at the school to respond to the FBV requirement, but that he was thinking of installing a Union-Jack-themed display in the foyer as that would "tick a box really", an instance of 'doing without believing' (Braun and Maguire, 2018).

Such decoration introduces a second, more maximalist version of *Representing Britain*, which uses British symbols to represent or 'imagine' the nation (Benedict Anderson, 2006). This approach was recently criticised by Ofsted's Chief Inspector of Schools when she argued that 'crafting a picture of the Queen out of sequins' was 'charming' but 'not teaching children about our common values' (Spielman, 2017). However, despite this and previous similar signals from Ofsted, it is an approach that still persists, a satisficing response that lends itself to stereotypes of 'Britain' and 'British' symbols and customs, which are made to stand for values (Arthur, 2015; Struthers, 2017).

Although, as noted earlier, the case study schools in this research did not primarily take up an approach to FBV which rested on 'British' symbols, there were instances of this (see Bamber, 2018b; Habib, 2018; and Sant and Hanley, 2018 for further examples of this response). A teacher at Kenton

Secondary suggested that visiting Shakespeare's Globe theatre in London and an opportunity for students to have a reward afternoon tea with the headteacher, with tea drunk from china cups, both counted as British values promotion, and the headteacher at Newton Primary put forward taking children to a pantomime. The headteacher at Garden Primary described the use of 'British' symbols as "tokenistic" but also said: "We have done a bit of that. Because we know people come to visit and they do expect to see some signs of it."

One common commercially produced poster, used in schools and aimed at young children (below eight years) features several boxed texts, stating 'we learn about …' and then listing 'British foods', 'British artists', 'British music' and 'British festivals'. It also includes headings dedicated to the general socialisation of young children ('we take turns and share', 'we are quiet and gentle', 'we practise our table manners'). The poster is decorated with pictures of the Queen, a red phone box, a Union Jack and the Houses of Parliament, with a red bus in the foreground. 'British food' is listed as 'roast dinner, cottage pie, vegetables from the garden, seasonal fruit, strawberries, scones, pasties, fish chips and peas' (with one regional variation featuring haggis, neeps and tatties). The British festivals listed are traditional festivals – the patron saint's day of the four nations of the UK, with the others being a mix of secular and religious celebrations, including Christmas, Easter, Pancake Day, Bonfire Night, Harvest Festival, Trooping of the Colour, Remembrance and Burns Night (but, oddly enough, not Halloween, which is widely celebrated by children in the UK but may have been seen as too American in its heritage). There is a box dedicated to 'we learn about the world around us' which includes 'we learn to respect people who are different' and 'we *mark* special multi-cultural days from our local community and the wider world' (emphasis added). This contrasts with another boxed text, that claims 'we *celebrate* British festivals' (emphasis added) – all of which suggests that difference is 'not us', not the British. Clearly, the difficulty with this poster and similar examples of the *Representing Britain* approach is that particular objects, behaviours and people are positioned as 'British' and so others by extension must be not British, a quietly exclusionary logic. How do young children receive such information? Are they not British if they don't eat 'British' food?

In Chapter Two, I noted Miller's description of the boundaries of a liberal nationalist shared public culture, which he notes should leave room for different private cultures: 'Thus the food one chooses to eat, how one dresses, the music one listens to are not normally part of the public culture that defines nationality' (1995: 26). The *Representing Britain* response reveals the ethnic nationalist underpinning of an apparently liberal nationalist policy. Although some research suggests teachers' discomfort with patriotism in schools (e.g. Jerome and Clemitshaw, 2012), the abundance of Union Jacks on display suggests that many teachers feel comfortable with a patriotism–lite, featuring the Queen and the achievements of famous (often White and male) 'British' people. Moncrieffe and Moncrieffe's study of the visual imagery in 27 primary school display boards on British values claims that over 80 per cent of the displays focused not only on cultural symbols but also on ones that deployed 'ethnocentric White British identities and histories to represent notions of fundamental British values' (2019: 59). They describe one display board's 'images of Queen Elizabeth the second; the red routemaster London Bus; a cup of tea; Winston Churchill, William Shakespeare; John Lewis (a department store) and a bulldog' (p. 53). This monocultural imagery is the reinvention of an imaginary past (e.g. celebrations of Empire Day).

Arguably, the avalanche of Union Jacks on school display boards was a preliminary response, with teachers being uncertain of how to respond to the requirement to promote British values, especially given the lack of guidance as to how to do so. Indeed, Shire School's preliminary response was along these lines, before teachers deemed it "tokenistic". However, the British values displays persist, and one primary school in the north-west of England recently claimed that holding a re-enactment of the wedding of the Duke and Duchess of Sussex (May, 2018) "ties in with our work on British values", again confusing a popular British icon – the Royal Family – with political and social values. My argument is that this response on the part of schools is an illustration of the extent to which, in many school sites, an emphasis on heritage and on traditional cultural symbols and practices is generally understood as unremarkable and so embedded into the fabric of schools' repertoires that it often passes unnoticed. These are examples of banal or everyday nationalism (see Chapter Two) where celebrating traditional symbols of the state is regarded as a quotidian part of a school's mission. For example, teachers at Newton Primary described the school's celebrations for the Queen's ninetieth birthday, a relatively common celebration across English primary schools in June 2016.

'We never used to have like community celebrations and things like that [but] we had the Queen's birthday last year, we made it a big thing in our school … We organised … like a tea party and then each class was asked to sing a song. So we all had to practise a song for each year group … mainly British songs that kindle patriotism or something like that … And we did mugs as well. We painted [them] and we did loads of activities related to the Queen's birthday and we had a lunch especially for the Queen … A fun day for the whole school, yes it was really nice.' (Nikita, Newton Primary, urban area, multiethnic, predominantly working-class population)

'You know we taught the kids *Jerusalem* … when we did the Queen's Jubilee or birthday – whatever happened this year for the Queen, … *Land of Hope and Glory*.' (Anika, Newton Primary)

In creating a lively and unusual day – all the school together in one space (this rarely happened as the school is large) – a day that has been planned and prepared for, the children's excitement at an out-of-the-ordinary event is harnessed through different affective modes: music, food and art. This allows the children to enjoy the event without perhaps fully understanding why they are having a tea party for the Queen. Yet the event is also generative of banal or everyday nationalism. As Billig says, 'the constant news about royalty provides inhabitants of the United Kingdom with banal reminders of nationhood, because it reminds them regularly of the family which symbolically represents that nationhood' (1992: xii). Such events, I suggest, disseminate subtle messages about Britishness. It fixes a traditional 'British' cultural symbol – the monarchy – as important enough to disrupt the school's normal routines and to invest time and energy in. The celebration fitted with the ethos of Newton where teachers, unusually among the multiethnic case study schools, emphasised a range of traditional British customs and Christian religious traditions (I observed assemblies on Lent and Advent, in compliance with the – often overlooked – requirement to have a daily worship of a 'wholly or broadly Christian' character) and talks about famous Britons (e.g. Winston Churchill and Prince Charles) also featured on the assembly rota. Learning about these traditional British symbols was positioned by staff as part of a multicultural curriculum, which also included assemblies on famous figures from other countries (e.g. Gandhi and Martin Luther King Jr) and international week (where each class adopted and learnt about a country), but it seemed to me that the British element dominated, and the head commented that "I lead quite strongly on the sense of being British and celebrating that". Arguably, the senior leadership team were concerned to teach the children whose heritage was mainly in South Asian, African and Eastern European countries, and who may not be familiar with or have access to knowledge about these traditions, about 'being British'. However, Britishness is presented as something fixed and static, something that students learn about from the outside, which is apparently not amenable to change. Their own contribution to Britishness as, for example, British individuals of South Asian heritage is not considered. This is an instance of what Suvarierol describes as 'nation-freezing': 'Practically, nation-freezing involves activities of the nation-state to reconstruct national identity through a new nationalist discourse that defines the elements of this "national culture" as if it was (ever) unitary and static ... A nation that would like to conserve itself in a particular idealised form' (Suvarierol, 2012: 212). Suvarierol is writing about 'citizenship packages', the information given by national governments to new migrants to prepare them for life in a new country. He comments that, compared to the Dutch and French equivalents, the British material (the *Life in the UK* book) specifically recognises the diversity of cultures and cultural practices that make up Britain (an example of the desire to promote oneself and/or the state as tolerant of difference, as described in Chapter One). However, the examples discussed here of 'imagining the nation' (Benedict Anderson, 2006) *do* present examples of nation freezing in classrooms across the country. This representation of 'Britishness', one that is taken for granted and quotidian, provides a landscape and a vocabulary for responding to the requirement to promote FBV, and which, despite Ofsted's misgivings, seemingly excludes the need for other approaches or responses. It is considered quite unremarkable for state schools, especially primary schools, to hold tea parties for the Queen, to have a special day's events to celebrate a Royal marriage or to hold commemorative ceremonies based on military traditions (as one of the case study secondary schools did). This acceptance illustrates the 'everyday performance of the nation by ordinary people' (Skey and Antonsich, 2017: 330) – ordinary people, in this case being the teachers who plan such events – 'the doxic, uncritically taken-for-granted everyday life' (Calhoun 2017: 18); the almost-universal "deep logic" that pervades our "common-sense" understanding about belonging and not belonging' to a nation (Billig, 2017: 317). As Silk notes, 'we need to understand how the use of heritage is imbued with power relations … and legitimates power structures by symbolizing who belongs in specific places' (2011: 739). The example of the commemorations of the Queen's birthday at Newton Primary shows that teachers, without mentioning 'British values', offer examples of what it means to be a 'good' British citizen and what knowledge is required.

My argument is not whether or not such events should be marked in schools. The Royal Family is currently very popular in Britain and is commonly equated with the nation (Billig, 1992: 34). Such celebrations can be joyful occasions, as the respondents at Newton described. The seeking out of commonality with others and the sharing of the bodily experiences of singing, playing and eating may lead to a sense of belonging born out of shared participation. However, I am interested in the extent to which such events are both ordinary and special, that traditional White British cultural heritage is taken for granted – not everywhere and always, but in many places and often – as the focus of special events. As examples of everyday nationalism, such events reveal the extent to which established ethnic groups (class differences are largely erased in this presentation of a 'fantasy' of unified Britishness: Bridget Anderson 2016) are in control of defining national identity and modes of behaviour that signal belonging. These moments of affective citizenship are not formal lessons, but they still generate messages about Britishness for students – what that entails, who is easily included and who is more marginal (see also Habib, 2018; Revell and Bryan, 2018).

Thus, to summarise: the *Representing Britain* response presents the idea that Britishness is unchanging, is about particular behaviours and attitudes and is not amenable to variation or open to diversity. This form of response to the FBV requirement draws on an embedded layer of ethno-cultural nationalism. That this ethno-culturalism appears so established, accepted and unremarked upon reveals the limitations of both a supposedly civic nationalism, where belonging is based solely on commitment to political principles, and its liberal variant where a 'thin' shared national identity provides a communal basis (see Chapter Two). These images of Britishness are both banal and trite on the one hand and powerful and exclusionary on the other, leaving little doubt as to who belongs in White Britain.

Repackaging FBV

The majority of teachers in my research rejected the *Representing Britain* approach. Teachers in the multiethnic schools especially felt that teaching children that 'Britishness' is a bounded space with a narrow range of characteristics could be divisive.

> 'And I think we were kind of looking at the use of the flag and stuff like that and what connotations that might have ... I think the fact that we have so many people from other countries, I don't think anyone would question the values ... themselves, but then ... we had seen some other posters that other schools had done. I think the flag bit just sort of stuck out for us ... We wouldn't necessarily call them 'British' values to the kids.' (Frank, senior leader, Kenton Secondary, urban area, multiethnic, working-class population)

> 'Like a return to the 1950s ... reductionist and crass ... When I see Union Jacks in a school, it breaks my heart a little.' (Laura, headteacher, Southern Primary, urban area, multiethnic, predominantly working-class population)

Likewise, a senior leader at Moreton Grange Secondary Academy described a "ridiculous assembly on fish and chips" that she had observed elsewhere. Shire's headteacher had encouraged a move away from the initial response of a display board for each FBV, seeing that as tokenistic: "For me it is about embedding that understanding that we are all different and we are all the same and we are all one community" (Diane, headteacher, Shire Primary, suburban area, mixed social class, White British population).

In response to such concerns, most of the schools in my research *repackaged* their existing activities. Auditing and emphasising current practice is recommended by those who offer support and training with FBV, and this process demonstrates schools' capacity to absorb the FBV policy (see e.g. The Key, 'Doing SMSC'[1]). Thus, schools offer their existing practices as evidence of the promotion of FBV; for example, the school council provides opportunities for the practice of democracy; the rule of law is covered by following school rules and individual liberty by learning to make 'good' choices.

I argue that *Repackaging* has many positive aspects in comparison to the *Representing Britain* approach. Focusing on school practices as manifestations of the FBV allows schools to present them to children as concrete, lived practices rather than as theoretical abstractions or abstract images. It also allows schools to smooth the potentially sharp nationalistic edges of fundamental British values, to 'filter out some of the muscularity of the imposed duty' (McGhee and Zang, 2017: 12; a reference to ex-Prime Minister David Cameron's 'muscular liberalism': see Chapter One). Teachers do this, McGhee and Zhang argue, by ensuring the maintenance of more inclusionary discourses 'respecting diversity and difference' (2017: 12), consistent with their existing aims.

To a certain extent, I agree with McGhee and Zhang. The schools in my research strongly emphasised 'respecting diversity and difference' through a broad commitment to multiculturalism, equality and mutual respect. This was evidenced in a wide range of curricular and other activities and institutional arrangements, including:

- enrolling the school in schemes such as UNICEF's Rights Respecting Award (Downs Secondary and Garden Primary), Stonewall School Champions (Valley High), and Show Racism the Red Card (*Union Primary*[2]);
- teaching ground rules for respectful debate through initiatives such as the school council (in all the schools, although some councils were more active than others), Philosophy for Children (Newton Primary and Kenton Secondary), Model UN[3] (Valley High and *Albernay*) and Jigsaw (PSHE materials used in Shire Primary);
- PSHE and RE schemes of work (including extended curriculum work on the Holocaust taught at Downs Academy, and 'No Outsiders' (Moffatt, 2011), a series of picture books and lesson plans to help schools respond to the spirit of the Equality Act 2010, used at Garden Primary);
- school ethos (leaders at Southern Primary, in particular, stressed staff modelling respectful interactions, and explicitly taught and assessed children on a range of values (staff elsewhere often focused assemblies on how to treat others);
- 'multicultural manifestations' (Joiko, 2019), including artefacts; recognising festivals from different religions; participating in special events such as Black History Month or Refugee Week; international days and weeks (e.g. at Shire and Newton children learnt about different countries) and international evenings (at Southern, parents brought food from their country of origin); and curricular initiatives (e.g. introducing the 'Golden Age of Islam' as a history topic at Downs so that students had some historical knowledge of Islam other than the Crusades).

All these examples illustrate teachers' concern to promote respect for others.[4] What was less evident, however, was comprehensive programmes of citizenship education. As discussed in Chapter Two, citizenship education is, at the time of writing, a marginalised subject in schools. However, initiatives did exist.

A common theme in the primary schools (Garden and Southern especially) was the use of 'Identity' to discuss citizenship (of a school, a locality, a country and the world). All of the case study secondary schools taught citizenship as a thread within PSHE (rather than as a separate subject), sometimes clearly badged as such and sometimes more diffuse. The topics largely focused on political literacy, such as knowledge of political parties, voting, and representative democracy. Popular activities were designing students' own political party and manifesto and/or a form of government for a desert island. I suggest that such work on political literacy is necessary but not sufficient for citizenship education, and this is discussed further in Chapter Five.

The initiatives outlined here can also be criticised for a degree of superficiality. This is a challenge long directed at multiculturalism for its 'saris, samosas and steel bands' approach (Troyna, 1993), which celebrates the exotic and colourful while leaving the quotidian operations, expectations and attitudes of the school and its staff untouched. The same point can be made of many of the other initiatives listed. Arguably, none of the areas that researchers argue are the source of current educational injustices – institutional racism, pervasive low expectations of some minoritised children and the badging of others as 'model minorities' (see e.g. Archer and Francis, 2006; Bradbury, 2013; and Rollock et al 2015), the marginalisation of working–class children (see e.g. Reay, 2017) and the surveillance of Muslim children through Prevent (Mac an Ghaill and Haywood, 2017) – are fundamentally challenged or unsettled by these 'respecting diversity' initiatives.

School councils: promoting the FBV of democracy?

One popular form of repackaging was for schools to signal the existence of a school (student) council as evidence that the school was promoting one of the FBVs: democracy. Initiatives in student voice are commonly considered to be inherently and uncomplicatedly positive (Teague, 2018: 98), although academic research presents a more cautious view, highlighting the gap between consultation and participation, and questions around the status of the council (who decides the agendas and which students are likely to be heard), to the extent that the entire exercise can seem like a lesson in the limits of representative democracy rather than its possibilities (e.g. Noyes, 2005; Whitty and Wisby, 2007).

In order to learn more about the degree to which school councils promote the FBV of democracy, I visited six of the nine schools to observe three primary and three secondary school councils (Shire, Garden and Newton primaries, and Moreton Grange, Holy Church and Valley High secondaries). My observations were differently organised by the schools. At most of the schools, I observed a school council meeting and had a short time to talk to the children (as requested). At Moreton Grange, I met with the council without a teacher being there but did not observe a formal meeting, and at Holy Church I observed a long meeting and then spoke with the head girl. The children and young people involved were all impressively articulate. The schools varied somewhat in the size of the school council and their modes of operation (e.g. the degree of involvement of the linked teacher, for example, and whether the school council had a direct link to senior management). Topics, however, were fairly uniform across the councils with 'toilets and chips' (Whitty and Wisby, 2007: 312) issues dominating; food, toilets, break-time behaviour and facilities, charity fundraising, mobile phone policies and the awarding of merits/detentions (the latter two being secondary school issues) were common. The representatives were often judged by the staff and the school council members themselves to be what one teacher referred to as the "good kids". At a meeting at Shire Primary, a 10-year-old girl earnestly explained that there were only girls present as the boys preferred playing football. The councils seemed to fulfil three main regular functions: students could offer input on new and existing behaviour policies and practices; staff could explain the rationale for these; and students could take on an active citizen role, raising money or contributing towards new initiatives (at Garden Primary, the school council had visited other schools to collect ideas for planning a new playground space). One school council meeting unusually addressed all three of these functions. I shall focus on it in some detail here because I believe that it offered students, in effect, an experience in the limits of democracy in schools.

Holy Church (urban, multiethnic, working class), a faith school, had closed over the summer after my first visits and reopened as part of a MAT. The school was to have a new headteacher, who was working at one of the other MAT schools. Some members of the school council had been to this academy and were reporting back to the council and the linked teacher, Jay. The students were unhappy about the more stringent procedures that they had witnessed (compared to those they were used to): stricter school uniform rules and a system for school lunches which included a ban on students bringing a packed lunch from home. Jay clearly had a good rapport with the young women[5] and talked with them in a calm, personal and gentle tone. His message, however, was that the students would have to capitulate and that their demands were unreasonable:

'Rules make you stronger and a better person. I know you are concerned about freedom – 'what about my life?' We are not turning you into robots. I love it that you are free-thinking individuals who are not afraid to speak your mind. I don't want to lose that. But these little things [in this case, the wearing of plain black school shoes] affect your academic achievement.' (Field notes)

The students conducted (and were allowed to) a long discussion about the organisation, pricing policy and limited choice offered by the lunch system they saw in action. Jay responded, "It's all about you. He [the incoming head] won't just not ask you [for feedback on new initiatives]." He advised them not to put up a "brick wall" straightaway: "You can't say it's rubbish if you haven't tried it" – in response to the idea of compulsory school lunch. On some points he had no response. Several students pointed out that packed lunches can work out cheaper to provide than £2.20 a day for school food.[6] But the policy was going to be implemented regardless of the views of the students or the teachers, a point he recognised when he said that they were now all "part of an academy chain that have their systems and we have to become part of that". There was no space for dissent. As Holy Church (before academicization), the school had been undersubscribed and staff members spoke of the small, but tight-knit, caring community. Jay sought to maintain and further build on this self-image, encouraging student commitment, but negating the force of their dissatisfaction by presenting it as a positivity: "This all tells me that you care a lot [about the school]. It is really useful information. We are a community [he pretended to sob and the students laughed]. But it's true" (Field notes).

I suggest that the school councils are a moment of 'everyday citizenship' (Tammi and Rajia, 2018: 627), and as such reveal the limits of the democratic power of students as citizens of the school. The unusual circumstances of the council meeting at Holy Church reveal the hierarchy of power. Despite claims about school councils enabling the student voice, facilitating students having a stake in decision making and allowing them to see the power of democracy, these students are being (gently) brought around to the position that their views are likely to be of little effect. The processes they disagree with are rolled out in all the schools in the chain, and *will* be happening in theirs. In a neoliberal education system with little room for teacher, student or parent representation, the take-over by the academy chain was agreed above the heads of both staff and students. Jay, although sympathetic to the students' concerns, encourages them to act in a mature, responsible fashion, to use the channels open to them (the new headteacher's possible desire for feedback) to express their concerns, but also to work on themselves so that they no longer *have* concerns.

To summarise: *Repackaging* is a response that acts to largely 'absorb' FBV into schools' already existing practices and procedures – a business-as-usual response. Importantly, this does avoid the sharply nationalist and exclusionary edges of the *Representing Britain* response. Additionally, teacher-respondents' commitment to developing students' sense of mutual respect was clear in the case study schools. This commitment has a longer history than the FBV requirement and is an instance of policy sediment, influenced by a history of (rather amorphous) commitments to tolerance, equality, fairness and multiculturalism, a point taken up in Chapter Five. I have also argued with regard to school councils – a popular way of repackaging the requirement to promote democracy – that such activities may be providing students with a lesson in the *limits* of representative democracy. An emotive commitment to symbolic democracy is signalled by the existence of school councils, but the experience seems to offer students few significant opportunities to exercise any power in the government of the school through their representatives.

Relocating FBV

The third approach – *Relocating FBV as school values* – is another form of absorption. This differs from *Repackaging* as it describes relocating and absorbing FBV within other work on values. While having a school motto and a series of desired aims expressed as values is common, schools vary in the degree to which they actively seek to instil particular values and modes of behaviour in students (the latter known as values/character/moral education, as terminology differs). Recent survey research suggests that schools' identification of 'character traits' that are important to them include both 'performance virtues' (Jubilee Centre, 2017: 1) such as perseverance and resilience, and 'moral virtues' such as tolerance and empathy (White et al, 2017: 6). Character education's popularity may derive from it drawing on and responding to an undefined and generalised conceptualisation of well-being and the development of 'soft skills' alongside academic skills. Thus, it becomes positioned as a commonsensical 'good thing', which is beyond the possibility of critique.

From the nine case study schools, the headteachers at Garden and Southern primaries claimed to disseminate a particular set of values (e.g. respect, resilience) throughout the schools' practices; in the case of Southern, teachers taught and assessed the school values explicitly, and the senior leadership saw them as integral to the operation of the school (see Vincent, 2018a for discussion). Other case study schools ranged from those that sought to promote a clearly identified range of values through assemblies and PSHE lessons, to those with a less clearly defined values base.

The increasing prevalence of values teaching in schools is one aspect of the school context often overlooked by the literature on Prevent and British values. However, I suggest that it is relevant, as the focus of this teaching tends to be on developing the self, rather than the self's relationship with society. Although the prevalence of 'respect' does signal an emphasis on social relationships, character education pays relatively little attention to students' understanding of the wider world, except in the form of 'civic virtues'. One influential organisation, the Jubilee Centre for Character and Virtue, defines civic virtues as 'civility, service, citizenship, and volunteering, which help students understand their ties to society and their responsibilities within it' (Jubilee Centre, 2017: 4). While such active citizenship is important in encouraging young people to appreciate the ties between themselves and others, it does not address skills in critical thinking and/or develop an awareness of social (in)justice, what Banks (2014) calls education for 'transformative citizenship' (or critical citizenship education: see Chapter Two).

I would contend that values education in the case study schools consists predominantly not of discussion of political and social principles (such as those of FBV) but rather of a focus on individuals working on themselves to strengthen their responsible and performative behaviours in line with neoliberal demands that the subject learn appropriate ways to govern the self. As Joseph comments with regard to resilience: 'Resilience fits with a social ontology that urges us to *turn from a concern with the outside world* to a concern with our own subjectivity …, our responsible decision-making' (Joseph, 2013: 40, emphasis added). The data include many examples of character education, but for reasons of space, I shall offer just two here, one primary and one secondary.

I start by focusing on one Jigsaw lesson (Jigsaw is a commercially produced PSHE scheme) that I observed with Year 4 (8–9 years) at Shire School. The children started by moving the furniture so that they had a circle of chairs. This physical movement signalled a different emotional tone to the session, a move to discuss feelings. However, the expansion of the boundaries of the normal tone – the classroom's 'emotional regime' (Zembylas, 2016b) – was actually quite limited, as the sessions focused on 'feeling regulation' – in this case overcoming disappointment. The children were given various scenarios that would induce disappointment and asked how the characters featured in them should react. They were then asked about experiences in their own lives where they had been disappointed, and also about the ways in which they cheered themselves up. The session was inclusive and conversational, and the children appeared to enjoy it greatly. Arguably, however, the session contained a particular set of expectations: just as the children were expected to improve their grasp of maths and English, this approach encouraged them to improve their grasp of their emotions. There was an implicit 'correct' emotional response, and a way of responding to emotions and managing the self, that were embedded in the conduct of the session – the readiness to name feelings and then overcome them – a lesson in the curriculum of a 'proper' emotional life.

In a PSHE session at Kenton Secondary with Year 10 (14–15-year-olds), a worker from an outside organisation sought to build personal resilience. Starting with a range of images to designate 'balance', 'resilience' and 'mental health', and asserting the particular vulnerability of this generation of students to stress and poor mental health ("The wider world of generation Z is not one of optimism"), the presenter went on to consider the sorts of emotions the children might experience at the time of transition (Kenton is an 11–16-year school so all students leave the school at 16), and then asked them "how they can learn to cope better in just 30 days" (a common time period for self-improvement plans such as diets or exercise programmes). The students were given a resilience grid with behaviours that had been "tried, tested and work to make you feel better" (expert, objective scientific knowledge is implied here: Nettleton, 1997), and then asked to set a personal resilience challenge. As the class became increasingly noisy, the presenter recommended that they include eating breakfast as one of their goals. Other resilience behaviours suggested included 'I use the library', 'I wear the correct uniform every day', 'I try hard in difficult subjects like language and maths', 'I understand the rules at school and keep to them' and 'I get to school on time', all of which were clearly goals that teachers find desirable and which appear to be more about student compliance than resilience. Ecclestone and Lewis, discussing similar resilience initiatives, aptly note the way in which a 'rules-based understanding of something as complex as resilience' fits into an educational context 'dominated by targets, criteria and performance measures' (2014: 201).

This type of initiative works to 'inculcat[e] techniques of emotional intelligence and emotional competencies into the emotional habits of each individual' (Zembylas, 2016b: 293), a development to which a focus on affect draws attention. 'Good' citizenship is here about encouraging children and young people to focus on themselves, to take responsibility for making wise choices about their behaviours in lessons, in school generally and in the rest of their lives; suggesting that their immediate futures (in terms of exam results) and their longer-term lives are for them to control, setting aside any recognition of structural barriers in favour of the 'notion of the active self' (Nettleton, 1997: 210; see also Kulz, 2017 for an analysis of the 'no-excuses' culture in one academy). The students at Kenton did indeed face structural barriers, with four fifths of the population from a minority ethnic group and over 70 per cent in receipt of 'FSM ever' (eligibility at any point over a period of six years for free school meals, a proxy indicator for poverty). While the school senior leaders were very aware of the pressures of poverty on the students, the focus of this particular session was on psychological processes. The students were assumed to be vulnerable in the face of several challenges listed in the session such as parental divorce, bullying and cyber-bullying; again the material context to the students' lives and possible poverty is not mentioned. In response to what are presented as psychological pressures, students are encouraged to develop psychological resilience, one element of which is presented as conforming to school rules, regulations and aspirations.

Thus, my argument is that, with the limited amount of curriculum time allocated to non-traditional subjects, the increased focus on character education crowds out citizenship education and the space the latter could offer for engaging with social and political principles, such as FBV. Within character education the most popular elements seemed to be the 'performance virtues', reflecting the influence of psychological theories and practices (Ecclestone and Lewis, 2014). This parallels the neoliberal trajectory Nettleton notes in relation to health, as individual patients, like individual learners, have been reconfigured from being passive recipients of knowledge to those who possess the capacity for 'self-control, responsibility, rationality and enterprise' (Nettleton, 1997: 214), so that the risk to a student's successful progress through school and later life is from him or herself (Nettleton, 1997: 214). Students are encouraged to act as entrepreneurs of the self, investing in and improving themselves, always with the promise of 'returns' in the future. The self, rather than wider society, becomes the focus of attention and activity. Such messages are not disseminated in a hectoring or even dispassionate manner, but rather the tone across the case study schools is one of gentleness, care and concern. It is, of course, possible that individual disciplinary interactions involved harsher tones, and that, as noted earlier, the institutionalised practices of schools continue to result in discriminatory practices towards certain groups.[7] However, the dominant tone of leaders and teachers in the research when discussing 'their' students demonstrates 'the vigour of care discourses within contemporary education markets' (McCuaig, 2012: 863), as schools promote themselves as respectful and safe spaces. This mode is constituted through what Foucault termed 'pastoral power'. Foucault argues that western states adopted and adapted pastoral power, a form previously associated with the Christian church, where the role of the pastor is fundamental in knowing intimately the lives and minds of his flock and guiding them towards salvation. In its modern form, pastoral power is 'no longer a case of leading people to their salvation in the next world, but ensuring it in this world. And in this context, the word "salvation" takes on different meanings: health, well-being (that is sufficient wealth, standard of living) protection against accidents' (Foucault, 1982: 784). He later notes that pastoral power in its contemporary form is a 'modern matrix of individualisation' (Foucault, 1982: 783), a technique for the 'production and conduct of governable identities' (Golder, 2007: 173). 'Pastoralism now aims not at salvation ... but at the government of life, health and well-being' (Curtis, 2002: 527). Schools, given their established institutional emphasis on the socialisation of the young, are a particularly likely site for the play of pastoral power. McCuaig cites Hunter (1994: xxi) on this point, who contends that it is 'Christianity's shepherd–flock game – with its distinctive articulation of surveillance and self-examination, obedience and self-regulation – that continues to provide the core moral technology of the school' (McCuaig, 2012: 865). She continues:

> It is this risky landscape with its neo-liberal emphasis on decision making ... that I suggest has contributed to ... an intensification of the pedagogical imperative for caring teaching. In their efforts to secure a productive and healthy citizenry, authorities' desire to know and shape the interiority of young people within the schooling apparatus has become of critical import. (McCuaig, 2012: 870–1; see also Ecclestone and Lewis, 2014)

To summarise, my argument is that *Relocating* is a response that subsumes FBV within values/character education. This shapes children's understandings of what it is to be a good citizen of the school – respectful, hard-working, persevering – and teachers hope to instil these values in students to the extent that they will use them to guide their present school life and their future adult life. These are all important values and behaviours, but are oriented inwards – towards developing 'good' people rather than 'good' citizens (Suissa, 2015). This is what Kisby calls 'personal ethics' rather than 'public ethics', focused more on how we should live, rather than on any engagement with social/political debates concerning how we should organise our social lives together (Kisby, 2017). The social and political principles of the FBV could – in theory – provide a basis for debating public ethics, but instead their enactment is relocated into values work that focuses on the self alone.

Conclusion

In this chapter, I have outlined three responses to the requirement to promote FBV: *Representing Britain, Repackaging* and *Relocating.* In the next chapter, I go on to explore the fourth response of *Engagement.* Here, I have identified the characteristics of the 'good' citizen identity that are inherent in the different responses, focusing both on the desired characteristics of the 'good' school citizen and the future 'good' adult citizen.

In the *Representing Britain* approach, the imagined community of the nation (Benedict Anderson, 2006) that comes into being through this set of resources is an unchanging nation which believes itself to be monocultural and monolingual – the preserve of the White British citizen (despite a multicultural gloss and the appearance of a few brown figures in teacher and student-made displays – a 'multicultural manifestation': Joiko, 2019). *Repackaging* – the majority response – avoids the nationalist emphasis of *Representing Britain*, but the absorption of the values into existing practices – the business-as-usual response – does not open up any new space for critical engagement with the values. Here, the FBV policy slides off the smooth institutional facades of audits and school councils, leaving little trace, and as a result many students will have only a fleeting encounter with the values (Healy, 2018). This then limits the likelihood that the policy will meet its apparent aim of students developing an informed commitment to FBV (a point further discussed later). I focused specifically on one of the most common ways in which schools repackaged the FBV, by claiming to promote democracy through a school council. I suggested that the experience of democracy for school council representatives (let alone the wider student body) was limited. The example of the Holy Church school council showed that, when major changes in the organisation and identity of the school were proposed, the students apparently had space to contribute (through the council), but their involvement was then limited to being heard but not listened to; that is, student representatives stated their views in the school council, and were then encouraged to work on their own emotions until they accepted all the forthcoming changes. *Relocating* the FBV into ongoing values work is another form of repackaging – although of a very specific kind. The moral and social development of the young has been and continues to be a long-established role for education. However, character education initiatives, focusing on personal, social and emotional development, command time and attention in schools, while citizenship education of any kind, especially a version that is focused on developing a critical political awareness, is much less prominent. Both the centring of values/character education and the marginalisation of citizenship education can be understood as acting to produce 'governable identities' among children and young people, in their roles both as 'citizens' of their current school and as future adult citizens of the nation.

Notes

[1] The Key: https://schoolleaders.thekeysupport.com/curriculum-and-learning/curriculum-guidance-all-phases/structuring-curriculum/promoting-british-values-in-the-curriculum/. Doing SMSC: http://www.doingsmsc.org.uk/british-values/ [Both accessed 9 May 2019].

[2] Italicised schools are those where I conducted just one interview.

[3] Model UN (United Nations) is a form of debating competition where young people adopt a particular country and research that country's likely attitude to a particular issue; debate then follows, in line with the structures of the United Nations. See https://www.una.org.uk/get-involved/learn-and-teach/model-un-portal [Accessed 9 May 2019].

[4] Much of this work relates to teachers' Public Sector Equality Duty (PSED) – although this was rarely explicitly referenced, and many initiatives had a history prior to the Equality Act 2010.

[5] As the school had become co-educational that term from Year 7, there were two 11 year old boys at the school council, but they said almost nothing.

[6] Families on state benefits are usually able to apply for free school meals (FSM). However, it is also possible to be on a low income but also ineligible for FSM.

[7] For example, Black Caribbean students were permanently excluded at nearly three times the rate of White British students in 2016–17 (DfE, 2018b).

FIVE

Morality, controversy and emotion in schools

The knowledge, skills, values and dispositions of hegemonic citizenship education discourses are not easily suspended as they are deeply rooted in the emotional ideologies of the nation. (Zembylas, 2013a: 15)

In Chapter Two I discussed the emphasis on 'making up' the 'good' school citizen and argued that this was a process shaped by an increasing emphasis on forms of character education which take a largely individualist, performance-focused approach. This chapter explores teachers' promotions of attitudes and values in relation to other individuals and wider society – what we owe to each other – and what teachers understand to be the affective range of feelings and attitudes held by 'good citizens', and their own emotions about the promotion of these values. The chapter has three main sections. The first discusses teachers' accentuating of mutual respect and tolerance when discussing FBVs, and what part that plays in their understanding of their professional role. I then discuss my fourth approach to FBV – *engagement* – and some of the difficulties and possibilities connected with it.

Finally, I consider which populations were understood by some teacher-respondents to be in particular 'need' of liberal values.

Teacher subjectivities

Chapter Three highlighted the direction of education policy in England which has emphasised competition between and within schools, target setting, teacher and school accountability for meeting those targets, and more traditional curricula and assessment methods (e.g. the recent large-scale removal of coursework from GCSE and A-level courses, the national qualifications taken at 16 and 18 years). Teachers are made responsible for policy but have no hand in shaping it. As Braun and Maguire (2018) note, the policy climate of constant and changing demands has produced what Ball (2003: 220) describes as 'ontological insecurity', where educators are beset by unease and uncertainty about what they should be doing, about meeting expectations and about what those expectations are (or will be in the next round of changes). 'As teachers engage with policy and bring their creativity to bear on its enactment, they are also captured by it. They change it in some ways, and it changes them' (Ball et al, 2012: 48). Braun and Maguire (2018) explore the impact of these changes, tensions and contradictions on teacher subjectivity. I discuss a small part of this larger topic here by focusing on teachers' sense of their role as moral agents.

Teachers as moral agents

Recent writing on teacher professionalism and subjectivity addresses how teachers respond to external accountability regimes, and the corresponding shift in the professional demands made of them. This shift has resulted in tension between a traditional 'thick' form of professionalism, emphasising the well-being and development of the whole child, and a newer 'thinner' form, stressing a child's progression through schooling in a linear manner, while achieving ever better test results (Moore and Clarke, 2016; Keddie, 2017; Braun and Maguire, 2018). These two imperatives indicate different understandings of the teacher, a traditional, perhaps idealised, one of an autonomous and creative professional, against an understanding, shaped by current policy directives, of an 'entrepreneurial' actor who welcomes external accountability and focuses on meeting targets (Keddie 2017). Researchers have illustrated the way in which teachers work to try to reconcile these competing subject positions, framed as they are by different narratives about who the 'good' and 'responsible' teacher is, and what they believe to be important. These studies describe, in slightly different ways, a balance struck, a hybridisation, the following of a 'logic of conformity' (Ball et al, 2012: 97) but perhaps 'without belief' (Braun and Maguire, 2018: 1). Braun and Maguire speak of 'pragmatic compliance' (2018: 8), Keddie of a mix of 'compliance and criticality' (2018: 210) and Moore (2018) of a 'virtuous pragmatism' (defined as a justification of compliance). Some teachers may view such settlements and the resulting practices with unease or 'discomfort' (Ball et al, 2012: 89–90), although Wilkins (2011) argues that many younger teachers can be understood as 'post-performative professionals', comfortable with balancing accountability and autonomy. Moore argues that individual teachers may continue to draw on traditional notions of professionalism – based on autonomy and trust – but that these are 'remaindered', and that current dominant definitions of professionalism focus on 'the prioritisation of individual and collective success in meeting measurable educational "targets" ... embedded within and supportive of a wider discourse and set of practices of performativity' (Moore, 2018: 103; see also Moore and Clarke, 2016).

My data suggest that one aspect of traditional professionalism that strongly persists is teachers' emphasis on their role in the development of moral behaviour towards others. The emphasis on holistic student development acts to allow teachers to balance their role in meeting targets within a competitive education system with a role in the development of 'good' citizens – both in young people's current lives as students of particular institutions and in their future ones as adult citizens. A majority of the teacher-respondents, across both primary and secondary schools, gave a clear account of their sense of responsibility to develop particular morals and values in their students in terms of how they treated others (see also Rowe et al, 2012). The goal of developing the whole person was often passionately, though rather vaguely, expressed. For example, in response to a question about the promotion of FBV, two teachers at Garden Primary said:

'If we think about British values, it is not just about famous men in history who have done something and Union Jacks. For me British values is more about promoting good morals and good attitudes ... it is more about teaching children life skills. And this is why it is important to tolerate people and actually it doesn't matter if, I don't know, most people centuries ago were Christian, but now this is what we are living in and actually it is diverse in the global community. So less [about] teaching the children to just put up Union Jacks. It is good for them to know that they are part of this country and this is the flag of the country and things like that but not that – I think it is important for them to have more of good morals, ethics ... So I guess in terms of what we are aiming for the British values to achieve is that the children are citizens.' (Rich, Garden Primary, suburban area, majority British Asian, mixed-class population)

'Maybe instead of saying 'British' values, [we should say] this is what it means to be a good person, this is what a decent human being would be doing, then in a way, that

would kind of make it more cohesive, not just within
Britain but globally.' (Meha, Garden Primary)

Similarly, Diane, the headteacher at Shire Primary
commented: "To me, [British values] is about looking after
everybody and valuing each other regardless of whether you
are British or not ... I think it is just about having values and
being morally a good citizen" (suburban area, mixed class, White
British population).

Interestingly here, these teachers acted in accordance with
their own sense of what it is to be a 'good' teacher, and translated
the FBV requirement to fit their own aims for educating young
children. Consequently, they focus on the explicit dissemination
of mutual respect and tolerance; indeed, Diane felt that with the
FBV requirement, "they [the government] have just given things
new names". Despite the absence of any direct questions from
me that singled out specific FBVs, teacher-respondents across
the sample emphasised their concern with mutual respect and
tolerance, 'developing the capacity to regard others as having
equal moral status and to treat them accordingly' (Clayton et al,
2018: 28), while the remaining FBVs tended to fade into the
background, addressed mainly by the existence of a school
council (to fulfil the requirement to promote democracy,
as discussed earlier) and in audits of practice. The focus on
mutual respect and tolerance (despite some teachers criticising
'tolerance' as limited: see Chapter Four) also allows teacher-
respondents to manage any discomfort they feel and to offer
some critique of those articulations of the FBV which offer
narrow, exclusionary versions of Britishness (as in *Representing
Britain*, a response which one teacher called "reductionist and
crass ... it breaks my heart a little": see Chapter Four). The
following quotes further illustrate the respondents' emphasis on
respect for and tolerance of difference:

'I don't say this is a British value that we will learn today, do you know what I mean? [I would say] we as a school, as a community, as a people, we respect and tolerate each other full stop. So I don't call it British values … I know they are British values but I don't necessarily say to [the students] "This is a British value", I just say "this is a core value that you should hold as a citizen". And that's it.' (Denise, Moreton Grange Secondary Academy, urban area, White British population, predominantly working class)

'No, I don't think we have [done anything differently to promote British values]. We have been doing what we have been doing for a long time … We live in a multicultural society [and] I would expect everyone to learn about all religions … learn and find out more about other people by what they think, what they believe, what they value, what they understand, and you respect everyone and respect isn't really [just a] British value.' (Annie, Newton School, urban area, multiethnic predominantly working-class population)

'And it is actually showing kids that: "look at our school now and how multicultural it is and in the class we are sitting in a room and we are all listening to each other. Isn't that a good value?" … It is the *right* thing to do.' (Dembe, Kenton School, multiethnic, working-class population, emphasis original)

'These are the values that can be found in all faiths, all schools, all communities: to respect and to be tolerant.' (Jacinta, Holy Church, urban area, multiethnic, working-class population)

These quotes suggest a similar response to that found by other researchers to the earlier requirement that schools work to promote community cohesion, whereby 'community cohesion' became a fulcrum for varied issues including citizenship, multiculturalism and 'getting along' with people (Phillips et al, 2011; Rowe et al, 2012; see Chapters One and Three). As discussed in Chapter Four, there is evidence of a heart-felt commitment among teacher-respondents to a rather nebulous set of values around equality of respect, drawing from earlier emphases on community cohesion and multiculturalism. Their focus is part of the hybridisation of professional priorities mentioned earlier, an emphasis that persisted alongside the expectations placed upon teachers in relation to student performance, and despite, in some cases *because* of, the tone of the broader political climate outlined in Chapter One. Although teacher-respondents did not all use the language of multiculturalism, the impact, the 'sediment' (Ball, 1994), of this older discourse, as defined here by Mitchell, was visible in their accounts, regardless of school demography:

> Multicultural education in liberal, Western societies is concerned with the creation of a certain kind of individual, one who is tolerant of difference, but a difference framed within certain national parameters and controlled by the institutions of the state. The subject interpellated through multiculturalism in education believes that cultural pluralism is good, or at least necessary, for national development, and is able to work with others to find sites of commonality, despite differences. (Mitchell, 2003: 392)

Multiculturalism, Mitchell argues, works to ' "perform" the liberal state and create a sense of a unified, tolerant and coherent nation' (2003: 391) but also to control difference, which is tolerated through the goodwill of the majority. Indeed, Mitchell's reference to the tolerance of difference 'within certain national parameters' should be read within the context of my earlier arguments (in Chapter One) about the narrowing of those parameters. In response, a few teachers directly expressed their concern about features of the wider political context that they felt had caused this narrowing, with reference to terrorism and hate crime, the presidency of Donald Trump and Brexit (see Farrell, 2019 on Brexit and FBV):

'But I worry that as we are departing from the EU and we are maybe becoming more of that island, then having something that is [badged] "British" values becomes more negative than positive because we are beginning to teach students about the fact that they are members of a community that is limited, when actually … the world they are going to be operating and working in isn't that way at all. So, I don't think it is helpful to have "British" as part of the values system.' (Will, Downs Secondary Academy, rural/suburban area, mixed class, mainly White British population)

These teachers were in a minority, though; most avoided any clear 'political'[1] statements (a positioning discussed further later in the chapter).

More generally, having *respect* as a normative value – its meaning assumed and unexplored, but publicised and embedded as a school value – helped teachers to negotiate areas of disagreement. Referring to criticism by a group of Muslim students of a school student Pride (LGBT+) group, Abigail at Kenton said:

'Actually, when you unpicked it, "well are you saying that people's beliefs and who they are shouldn't be respected?" When they [the critical students] started to think about it, they were like, "No, no that wasn't what I was saying". … So, it is about challenging that and having those discussions, those open discussions, and always going back to "we are a diverse community, we respect everyone within the community". And that is – we have got to hold true to that. And we have that moral responsibility.' (Senior leader, Kenton Secondary, urban area, multiethnic, working-class population)

This general arena of 'good morals', for a minority of the teachers, also included a clear emphasis on developing students' sense of their own political efficacy. For example, Charles, headteacher at Downs, talking about the school's Holocaust programme, noted that

'[Holocaust education] actually gives a child the chance to realise that they are a small part in a huge world but that they can influence it and they can do good and they need to do these things ... And it is so key, because too many children if they are capable of getting English and Maths A$\star$ to C^2, [in] five [GCSEs] they are treated like a little 'oh you are wonderful, you are great' and the reality is they are not, and they need to understand ... how awful things happen and how they can influence things.' (Rural/suburban area, mixed class, predominantly White British population)

Similarly, Joseph, the headteacher at Valley High, speaking at the start of a Model United Nations conference, asserted the value of promoting student voice, the power of the individual to make a difference and collective responsibility to make the world a better place: "the importance of 'us' as well as 'me'". He told students, "your voices matter, your experiences matter, your stories matter" (Field notes, Valley High, urban area, mixed class, multiethnic population). This emphasis on developing an independent, assertive public voice in young people was less commonly articulated in the primary schools, although a teacher at Garden Primary was a marked exception:

'My job is to encourage these children to speak up about the things they see, injustices, and so it is almost arming them for that really in terms of preparing them for those conversations that they are going to have. If they see things, I want them to feel confident to challenge it. ... You always emphasise the fact that [the classroom] is a safe environment to have those conversations.' (Joe, Garden Primary, suburban area, majority British Asian, mixed social class population)

The everyday promotion of mutual respect coexisted for the teachers with the demands of external accountability measures. These demands clearly shaped the context in which teachers enacted the FBV requirement. They were tangible and visible in several ways, for example, the palpable anxiety of leaders at Kenton Secondary around the school's latest Ofsted verdict of 'requires improvement'; the proliferation of FBV audits (several case study schools audited existing practices promoting FBV as 'evidence' for their next inspection); the ordering of the curriculum (e.g. senior leaders at *Point High* would not countenance the introduction of a Citizenship GCSE as it is not an EBacc subject); and a preoccupation with results and targets. On this last point, Charles, headteacher at Downs Academy, described the response to a 'dip in results':

'We got all sorts of slapped wrist-y things, just for this one dip. We are above national average, but we dipped from where we were and I had – the Regional Schools Commissioner[3] sent someone to check the school out. I had to go to a board of theirs – it was ridiculous. I told them it was just a blip. Then of course we got this stonking [i.e. exceptional] set of results [the next year].'

An FBV audit at Downs raised a number of further issues about the pressures of teaching within a performative climate. One teacher described the reasoning behind it as: "They [senior leaders] just wanted to cover all bases. That is kind of the school's mantra really. As an outstanding school they don't want to give anyone any reason to criticise." Another juxtaposed 'the audit and the truth', an example of how schools feel under pressure to continually document the best possible version of their activities. Such efforts clearly affect staff: another teacher commented that

> 'I think it is quite hard as a place to work because it is an outstanding school, so there is an awful lot of pressure and expectation which is difficult. I think that sort of striving to gain outstanding and be viewed as outstanding quite often means that other things fall behind, like staff well-being and things like that.'

These examples illustrate that the promotion of FBV is one policy among many that teachers are required to enact, and that the dominant policy demand is that of meeting individual and school targets for performance.

Discussing the shaping of teachers' subjectivities in such a context, Moore and Clarke argue that being a teacher involves working for 'impossible futures', a 'fantasy of equality of opportunity' (2016: 670), one in which every student attains highly, leaves school as a mature, reasonable adult/older child who respects and can work with others, and is ready to clearly articulate their own views. This aim also requires teachers to overlook their own roles in classifying students in myriad ways, that divide them into those who may fulfil their teachers' desire for their futures and those who will not do so (because of perceived deficits in their attainment, morality, values and/or behaviours). The difficulties associated with a project of 'impossible futures' are heightened by conditions of precarity and growing inequality in late capitalism (Moore and Clarke, 2016: 669–70). I suggest here that, for the teacher–respondents, articulating the importance of equality of respect and promoting that belief to students provided a set of investments beyond the 'thin' professionalism offered by meeting targets. The task may be an impossible one, but its undertaking has affective importance, that is, it offers teachers a sense of their work as bettering students' lives and improving society. Through teachers' dissemination of the liberal values of mutual respect and tolerance, they can meet their desire to send out not only young people with academic credentials but also those with morally good attitudes. Crucially, in terms of the affective work of such a mission, they can continue to claim this role of moral agent to be a result of their own 'thick' professional understandings – 'we were doing this anyway' – and not as a response to government edicts (Moore and Clarke, 2016; Keddie, 2018). I return to this argument in Chapter Six.

Engagement

My fourth response to the FBV requirement is *engagement* with FBV. This describes taking a critical approach to the values by, for example, looking at the advantages and limitations of democracy. Elements of this approach were adopted by some of the case study secondary schools but not systematically, and none followed an explicit programme of engagement with FBV. Rather, they tended towards absorption (as discussed in Chapter Four).

Ted Cantle, a researcher on issues of diversity and cohesion, has called for more 'dangerous conversations' in schools, which he defines as conversations that 'help young people to come to terms with all aspects of difference …, to build a wider acceptance of plurality' (Cantle, 2015: 12–13).[4] Similarly, the Department of Education states that citizenship education should 'equip pupils with the skills and knowledge to *explore political and social issues critically*' (DfE, 2013, emphasis added). Support for this comes from Jerome and Elwick's (2017) recent study, which demonstrates the appeal of learning about political and social issues for young people, and Habib (2018) discusses and illustrates the key role of critical art pedagogy in allowing students to reflect on national identity. In my own research, I asked teachers about potentially sensitive issues or 'dangerous conversations', and they identified the following: Brexit, terrorism, media representations of Muslims, relationships and sex education and same-sex relationships, and in particular, and for all the secondary schools in the research, immigration and migration. All these topics could involve discussion of one or more of the FBV, providing the content for what Bamber et al describe as a 'pedagogical approach that educates *through*, rather than *about* or *for*, FBV' (2018b: 445, emphasis original). In my research, there was some often partial and patchy engagement with these 'dangerous' issues. In the secondary and most of the primary schools, some discussion of Brexit had taken place with the students, together with some mock EU referenda. Teachers at all the schools had made some response to the 2017 terror attacks in England, holding assemblies or talking to the students in tutor time, aiming to reassure them. As will be further discussed, more systematic exploration of terrorism is included in the RE GCSE syllabi. However, in general there was limited engagement with these 'dangerous' issues. This was for several reasons, both practical and affective.

Limitations to 'dangerous conversations'

The *practical* reasons included the performative pressures on schools (discussed earlier) and the overwhelming focus on student performance in written exams and tests. Rose, a teacher at Valley High, argued that since skills in speaking and listening are no longer assessed as part of the English GCSE syllabus, the message to students appears to be "we value democracy, but we are not going to teach you how to speak". The lack of time for debate in a crowded curriculum, with pressures to get through the syllabus, was mentioned in all the case study schools. Furthermore, teachers may have had no training in discussing controversial or sensitive issues (Davies, 2018). They may be non-specialists teaching PSHE or citizenship sessions. Discussing contemporary political and social issues with children and young people is immensely demanding. As well as the mundane realities of everyday classroom management, teachers have to be well informed themselves in order to be able to understand and to respond to students' occasionally half-remembered references, and to be confident in participating in and managing discussions. There are issues here of neutrality, partisanship and ethics, and the long shadow of indoctrination. These are not simple matters that can be completely 'solved' through training, as they generate a series of *affective* responses – of unease and uncertainty – which, in addition to the practical time constraints, means that many teachers avoid and/or limit discussion of 'dangerous' issues.[5] Kibble (1998, cited in Oulton et al, 2004) speaks of 'dirty' issues, by which he means complex, but I find the label interesting. Getting your hands 'dirty' can mean getting involved in something dishonest, something that is unsuitable for professionals, something that lacks the clear 'purity' and straightforward nature of factual transmission to children. This affective unease works on two levels. There are some explicit limits regulating what can be said, as well as discursive limits on what would be 'thinkable' for the 'good' teacher.

In terms of *explicit limits*, the Education Act 1996 expressly forbids 'the pursuit of partisan political activities'. Teachers must promote FBV, and to speak against them is, according to Prevent duty guidance (Home Office, 2015: 5), a sign of extremism in a teacher or a student. The Public Sector Equality Duty (Equality Act, 2010) also requires teachers not to make overtly discriminating statements in the classroom on the grounds of race, sex, disability, sexual orientation or religion, and they have a duty to foster good relations between minority and majority groups. However, although the existence of regulation is clear, exactly what can be said in the classroom is less so. 'The legal, hegemonic and moral limitations' (Quartermaine, 2017: 550) on 'dangerous conversations' impose both a tight and a hazy grip on students and teachers. Limitations are felt and/or feared acutely, but their exact boundaries are unclear.

Although these two duties – Prevent and PSED – provided the statutory regulation to govern discussions, teacher-respondents mentioned them by name infrequently when speaking about controversial issues. Rather, they voiced two particular sets of concerns: how to respond to xenophobic attitudes, particularly likely, they felt, to be expressed around migration; and to what degree they should make their own views clear during discussions. The tension here was between promulgating mutual respect and tolerance, and feeling that they were – or could be accused of – indoctrinating students. Superimposed on both issues was a concern about being able to control the emotional tenor of a controversial discussion (see also Busher et al 2017). Don, a teacher at Downs Secondary, described decisions as to how much of his own opinions he could explicitly refer to as "walking a tightrope" (see also Hess, 2004). In contrast, but in a minority, Jacinta at Holy Church linked her view to her understanding of her role as a moral agent: "I don't think I have ever questioned whether I should put my opinions forward. I think I would be doing the girls a disservice if I didn't." Most teachers agreed on the need for "red lines" (Sam, Downs) concerning what students could say, although these were clearer for some than for others. In general, there was agreement on the unacceptability of overtly discriminatory comments on the grounds of race, religion or sexuality (in line with the PSED).

The difficulties of teaching controversial issues are not new. The Humanities Curriculum Project in the 1970s advocated 'procedural neutrality' as a solution, in which the teacher acts as a neutral chair of classroom discussions, encouraging students to listen and to reflect on others' views (Elliott, 1983; Cotton, 2006). Pykett (2007) notes that a discourse of neutrality is also built into the influential 1998 Crick Report on citizenship education (QCA, 1998: 27). However, exhortations to maintain balance and neutrality do not necessarily address teachers' concerns about where to draw red lines when discussing issues involving discrimination or prejudice. Aware of this requirement for 'balance', teacher-respondents explicitly spoke of the lengths they went to in order to avoid partisanship and its appearance in their teaching:

> 'Sometimes I am so careful of not giving my own view that I almost promote the things that I don't believe in. So, I am a member of the Labour Party and a keen Labour supporter, but when we are discussing the differences between the main political parties, ... I'm trying not to promote Labour too much. Trying to be neutral and actually probably going too much the other way, so it is really hard, I do think it is really hard. I sometimes wonder if it is just worth saying "Look this is where I stand", but I know it is difficult because kids are impressionable.' (Don, Downs Secondary Academy, rural/suburban area, mixed class, mainly White British population)

Sam, also at Downs, described how, in response to the students' interest in Donald Trump's 2018 proposed ban on citizens from particular countries travelling to the US, she put together a resource listing his critics' and supporters' rationales. In an attempt to be 'fair' she tried to put an equal number of points in each column, 'no matter how tenuous or ridiculous' she felt some of the points she made in favour of the ban were. At Valley High, where the local population was understood by all the staff I spoke with to be "very liberal/left-wing", teachers spoke of their concern to introduce students to more conservative views. Only one teacher in the sample, Alesandro at Holy Church, argued explicitly for the need to introduce a position directly critical of recent governments, stating that, in order to understand the present-day situation in the Middle East, "you also have to look at western politics", and adding, "As a so-called civilised western democracy ... you have got us contravening refugee international policies and things that we have signed up for. It is like pretty disgraceful. So, you do have to look at things from those points of view as well." (See later discussion of *Marina School's*[6] materials for teaching about terrorism.) Discussing anti-immigrant headlines in the right-wing press, Alesandro argued that "I am not trying to push an opinion but what I am trying to do is give people more of a choice. And coming to conclusions of their own rather than just being fed something." This teacher sees his role as offering balance by presenting an opposing view to those with which students are familiar (as at Valley High). Pykett argues that a common-sense emphasis on neutrality – posing arguments for and against – 'serves to naturalise power equalities and to re-inscribe them through supposedly neutral categories' (2007: 314–15), and this is reflected in the general hesitation from teachers to appear critical of the policies of any recent governments.

As well as practical, explicit limits outlined earlier, *discursive* limits to speech and thought shape teachers' practices. Thus, Judith Butler's concept of 'domains of the sayable' is useful here:

> The subject's production takes place not only through the regulation of that subject's speech but through the regulation of the social domain of the speakable discourse. The question is not what it is I will be able to say, but what will constitute the domain of the sayable within which I begin to speak at all. (Butler, 1997: 133)

Laura Teague uses this concept to explore the production of 'what it is possible to think and say in the official times and spaces of teaching and learning' (2018: 93). Teague argues that Butler's concept allows us to see censorship not solely as an external force, but as 'implicit, internalised' (2018: 104), through which particular subject positions are enacted. 'To move outside of the domain of speakability is to risk one's status as a subject' (Butler, 1997: 133); that is, for a good teacher, a professional, responsible teacher, being 'professional' is a term 'imbued with positivity' (Moore, 2018: 103). Moore also argues that the discursive understanding of a 'professional' is one compliant with the current culture of performativity, and that compliance is shaped by a commonly shared affective desire, to fit in, to be liked by colleagues, that he refers to as 'the allure of normalcy' (Moore, 2018: 109). Thus, the internalised force of what is sayable or thinkable means teachers avoid or limit 'dangerous conversations'. Moore adds that, although we may as individuals become consciously aware of the effects of discourse, this does not make it easier to act outside their frame (Moore, 2018: 104).

Strategies

Having discussed both the practical and the affective constraints that, I argue, explain why teachers limit and avoid controversial/sensitive issues, I now turn to look at the strategies employed when debates *are* scheduled. In order to keep discussions 'manageable', teachers act to temper the emotional climate of the discussion, and often spoke of introducing 'hard' facts, using data to restrain or preclude any outbreaks of emotion. Don describes how, in the run-up to the EU referendum, he responded to students voicing support for the migration policies of the right-wing party UKIP:

'I said to the kids, "There are issues around immigration, there is no getting away from it and we need to discuss those sensibly and maturely and once you have got the facts in front of you …" – because that is the problem I find sometimes with the whole thing of just saying what they have heard from their parents, they don't really understand the message, they are just repeating it … And I tend to approach it in that sort of empirical way, "Here are the facts and if you want you can do what you like with the facts as long as it is in that acceptable zone"[7] … So when the Brexit thing was all kicking off in the Referendum I did a whole PowerPoint presentation that was just on Britain's relationship with the EU and frankly it was quite a lot of me talking, this is what Britain pays into the EU, this is what Britain gets out of the EU … Then at the end we have a discussion about it.' (Don, Downs Secondary Academy, mixed class, predominantly White British population)

'Frankly it was quite a lot of me talking' suggests that Don remained in control of the emotional tone of the debate, which he deliberately muted. He positions the students as unknowing – lacking in particular data-based knowledge. Once they were handed that knowledge, the hope was that they would develop more liberal views. However, 'ignorance' may not be easily 'solved' by adding the missing knowledge. Ignorance can be driven by a 'deeply-seated epistemic resistance to [difficult] knowledge', what Zembylas refers to as 'wilful ignorance' (2017: 503). As well as the possibility of 'wilful ignorance', there is also anxiety over difference and diversity – over what can and may be said (Zembylas, 2016a). Anxiety may lead to a level of self-policing among both teachers and students, a sense of (self)-surveillance and therefore a desire to fit in with what can be deemed acceptable. Quartermaine, observing mainly White British students discussing terrorism, notes

manoeuvres witnessed during the group discussions, … when pupils made associations between terrorism and Islam but would then justify their statements by adding 'that's what we see in the news' or 'that's all we hear about' […] [These statements] ensured that the pupil felt he or she would not be considered prejudiced against Muslims. (2017: 547–8)

Similarly Bennett and Lee-Treweek (2014) point out that the silences they find when White British students are invited to talk about race and racism can effectively close down discussion, another form, perhaps, of 'wilfulness':

The uncommunicativeness of these pupils [in their study] and the use of the sweeping 'it's wrong isn't it' echo post-race discourse, which suggests that, as there is no issue, there is nothing to add or say. Moreover, the orthodoxy of there being nothing to say adds to teachers' difficulties in trying to tackle racism and diversity issues in classrooms, since they have no way of talking about it and there is no socially recognised need for it. (2014: 41)

'Pedagogies of discomfort'?

I suggest that, beyond explicit regulation, 'domains of the sayable' work to limit 'dangerous conversations' on diversity and difference to less contentious grounds. A very different view of what education is, or should be, for is put forward by Boler and Zembylas in their discussions of 'a pedagogy of discomfort':

[This is] a teaching practice that can encourage students to move outside their 'comfort zones' and question their 'cherished beliefs and assumptions' (Boler, 1999, p. 176). This approach is grounded in the assumption that discomforting feelings are important in challenging dominant beliefs, social habits and normative practices that sustain social inequities and they create openings for individual and social transformation ... Such a pedagogy has as its aim to uncover and question the deeply embedded emotional dimensions that frame and shape daily habits, routines, and unconscious complicity with hegemony. (Zembylas, 2015: 163, 166)

Chetty makes a similar point. In relation to Philosophy for Children, he observes that the development of 'reasonableness' is prominent among its goals, but argues that what appears 'reasonable' is socially constructed and that 'educators need to take active steps to bring in perspectives that are insufficiently represented, particularly when their under-representation may be related to historical oppression and marginalisation' (2018: 6). In focusing on a struggle against collective forgetting in relation to social injustices, he draws on Alexis Shotwell's (2011) idea of 'racialized common sense' to argue that common sense is the voice of the majority group that is often unaware of alternative understandings from minority groups. Chetty concludes that 'starting in a place that appears at first unreasonable might help us to perceive the historical and social processes that contribute to our conception of reasonableness' (2018: 13). This is about drawing out and making 'visible subjugated meanings and unsettle and open up to troubling, those meanings that inscribe the normative' (Code, 2007: 69) – a struggle against collective forgetting, particularly in relation to social injustices.

The teacher-respondents in this study took a different, simpler position than either Chetty or Zembylas (who also discusses ethical issues around 'pedagogies of discomfort'). When controversial issues *were* tackled, emotion was minimised through the use of formal debating structures, deploying 'hard' (and apparently neutral) facts and limiting debate to question-and-answer sessions (with the teacher thereby retaining firm control). A pedagogy of discomfort was absent from the data and that absence was both practical (e.g. lack of time) and affective (unease over what could and should be said; an understandable fear of allowing a discussion to spin out of control, and safeguarding concerns if students said hurtful things to each other). Such a pedagogy is also 'unthinkable' in the present educational climate where encouraging students to work on themselves is largely directed at their behaviours and aspirations around achieving at school (see Chapter Four).

To summarise: I have argued up to this point that teachers have a strong but amorphous commitment to developing 'good' young people, and this is expressed in terms of encouraging an attitude of equality of respect. This allows them to maintain a professional identity and practice in accordance with the demands of a performative educational climate, which requires them to divide and classify students, celebrating some and condemning others, while also drawing on long-established professional priorities about developing the whole child, thereby maintaining their role as 'thicker' and more fundamental than meeting targets; they are helping to mould good, moral beings. This hybrid identity, bringing together elements of traditional and current discourses of professionalism, is not necessarily a conscious strategy but one that produces a sense of self as an effective *and* caring professional. However, this effective and caring professional is not a disruptive one, and I have identified here both the practical and affective factors which act to restrict both the frequency of classroom discussions of controversial issues and the register of acceptable emotions in those that do take place. Next, I turn to a closer look at examples of teaching about terrorism, which illustrate the difficulties and complexities teachers face in addressing emotive topics.

Discussing terrorism

In order to explore the idea of engagement with controversial/ sensitive issues further, I observed lessons addressing terrorism in three secondary schools: PSHE lessons for Year 10 (14–15-year-olds) in Holy Church; RE for Year 7 (11-year-olds) in Moreton Grange Academy; and RE for Y10 in Kenton. In addition, I was given teaching materials from another two schools (*Marina Grammar* for Year 10, and Downs Academy, also aimed at Year 10). I make two main points here: the first is that a primary concern of all the teachers was to complicate and problematise the link which they perceived students may have made between 'Muslim' and 'terrorist', and the second is the lack of context and depth in some discussions of terrorism (for a different approach see Jerome and Elwick, 2017).

On the first point, the lesson I observed at Moreton Grange was the first in a block of lessons deliberately introduced into RE for Year 7 because the locality was thought by the teachers with whom I spoke to be 'insular' and wary of visible difference. In advance of the lesson, Val commented that her aim was to "correct [the students'] views". She also noted the need to be neutral. These are not necessarily contradictory views, because part of the PSED requires teachers to have 'due regard to the need to eliminate discrimination, advance equality of opportunity and foster good relations between different people when carrying out their activities' (Equality and Human Rights Commission 2014). The lesson started with the 'staircase of tolerance' running from 'hatred' on the bottom step to 'celebrating diversity' at the top and, after discussing the meaning of the various terms, the children were asked to identify the link between this activity and terrorism. One boy responded that terrorists have hatred for people, and another that the media have hatred for Muslim people. Val notes that "We all know terrorism is not related to one religion. 99.999 per cent of Muslims fight against terrorism". Similarly, at Downs Secondary, teaching notes from the citizenship lead teacher for tutors on a Year 10 hour-long input on religious extremism acknowledge that "it is highly likely" that some student comments "may be prejudiced towards one religion (Islam). Please allow these things to be said but challenge them through the use of the tasks which shows that religious extremism is not just within one religion but can be with any." Tutors are further encouraged to clarify that "Islam teaches peace" and that "extremists are not accepted by Islam". This is an example of an important intention to disrupt students' (presumed) prejudice, but one being undertaken in a somewhat squeezed and piecemeal fashion through a one-hour input. In similar attempts to challenge prejudice, teachers in several schools who related discussions about recent terror attacks with pupils (with the aim of reassuring them about the risks to their personal safety) were also keen to emphasise that the terrorists are not representative of Muslims in general, nor do they follow the precepts of Islam:

'I think members of staff are conscious that when they are talking about it there are students in the classroom who are Muslim, because a lot of it is coming from Muslim fundamentalists, and I always mention that it is not actually Islam what is happening, it is criminal and it is not Islam in terms of what the majority of people think, it is fundamentalists.' (Stan, Valley High Secondary, multiethnic, mixed social class population)

In view of the political context outlined in Chapter One, these efforts indicate teacher-respondents' commitment to challenging prejudice.

The second point in terms of the content of lessons on terrorism is to do with the difficulty of covering a broader historical and political context when discussing extremism and terrorism, including an 'examination of current inequitable circumstances that ostracize and marginalize certain groups' (Gereluk, 2012: 112). Student discussion of context was limited in my observations by lack of lesson time and of suitable content. Textbooks like the *OCR Religious Studies GCSE* textbook (Abbot and Clarke, 2016), used in Kenton School, addresses terrorism in just a few pages. A senior leader at Kenton commented that staff had to start by unpicking the 'coupling' she perceived in the text between Islam and terrorism. Indeed, the section starts with a picture of the burning Twin Towers, and the first substantive topic is 'Islamic extremism' which mentions FBV as part of the British government's counter-terrorism strategy. The textbook then moves to Christian terrorism, with a case study of the IRA, and a mention of an Indian Christian terrorist organisation. The chapter ends with a discussion of just war theory.

When this material was taught to a Year 10 class, the teacher, Dembe, did not use the textbook immediately. Aiming to illustrate that terrorism is a wider phenomenon than Islamist extremism, she asked students to identify various pictures of historical and contemporary attacks. She stated that not all terrorism is religious, and played a BBC video about the Northern Ireland 'Troubles', about which only one student had heard. The content offers a succinct account of the war and ends with the 1998 Good Friday Agreement, noting that 'dialogue, not violence, is the way to achieve a lasting peace'. Interestingly when she asked for reactions, a girl commented that terrorism used to be about politics but is now about religion, and a boy, presumably understanding the BBC account of the Troubles to be one of straightforward closure, said that terrorism was more easily resolved in the past than the present. Dembe counteracted the last view, but there was no time for more discussion as the lesson moved on to the idea of a just war. This vignette illustrates the effect of lack of context and time, which can result in partial student understandings and misinterpretations. Despite the teachers' impulses to promote mutual respect and tolerance, their efforts can also be seen as a satisficing response at the level of policy and practice. Teachers are required to promote FBV and to bolster students' resilience to extremism, and so teaching about terrorism is squeezed into the curriculum.

I saw two sets of material that did develop a historical and political context to the discussion of different terrorist movements. One was from *Marina*, a grammar (academically selective) school, where a block of six lessons on global terrorism was taught to Year 10 students. In interview, the headteacher, Elliott, emphasised the use of "hard-hitting material", with an emphasis on contemporary events. The *Marina* resources included more material on Islamist than other forms of terrorism, although again they included the message that Islamism is 'detached from mainstream Muslim thought and theology, indeed Islamist extremists have perpetrated the same violent acts towards many Muslims as they have towards non-Muslims'. The material includes the notion of contested and changing definitions of a 'terrorist' and a 'freedom fighter', and looks in detail at case studies of Boko Haram in Nigeria and of the IRA, radicalisation, counter-terrorism and the tension between security and civil liberties. Students also had to choose and research a terrorist group independently. In a lesson on Islamist terrorism, the written material asks students, among other questions: 'What in your opinion are the root causes of Islamic extremism? Does the West hold any responsibility for the growth of Islamist terror organisations? If so, in what way(s)?' This gives an indication of the greater depth in which these issues are treated, compared to most of my other examples. The material was also text heavy in comparison to that used elsewhere, as staff felt students at *Marina* were skilled at absorbing and processing written information.

A different, but also in-depth, approach came from Holy Church during PSHE, taught by Alesandro. Year 10 students started the first in a block of lessons by drawing their image of a terrorist in order to explore stereotypical depictions. Then they were presented with the fictional story of potential terrorist Bobo living in a refugee camp after his family had to flee their (fictional) country after an invasion. Bobo's story is entitled 'a narrative of hate', and students were asked to identify the pieces of a jigsaw that led to Bobo's radicalisation. The class identified feelings of loss, grief and trauma after a brother's death; humiliation at the hands of soldiers; loss of land and home; feelings of hopelessness; the craving for power and desire for revenge. Alesandro added to their suggestions the propaganda of those doing the radicalising. The lesson sought to create an empathetic understanding with the disenfranchised, would-be terrorist, who remains a sympathetic figure as, at the end of the story, he renounces terrorism without harming anyone. The materials for the following lesson, which I did not observe, suggest that the students go on to discuss whether such an optimistic ending is realistic.

The contrast between the two approaches is clear. The teachers are responding to what they understand to be the academic orientations of the students at the two schools, with Alesandro at Holy Church emphasising visual approaches such as mind maps and the use of art work. It is an affective approach and contrasts with the more cognitive approach of the materials from *Marina Grammar*'s citizenship lessons. This may be an uncomfortable difference when we consider that *Marina* is a selective boys' school with a mainly middle-class, ethnically mixed, but majority White British population, whereas Holy Church attracted a predominantly working-class, mainly Black, female population. However, both schools had teachers and senior leaders who considered it worth investing considerable time in creating resources to teach about terrorism in a way that adds nuance, complexity and detail to the students' understanding. Thus, these examples demonstrate the possibilities of 'dangerous conversations' (see also Jerome and Elwick, 2017). As Davies (2018) concludes in her study of education and counter-extremism, the emphasis should be on building 'a permanent culture in schools where resilience to extremism is just one aspect of a fuller learning of rights, history, religious and ethnic conflict and community dynamics' (2018: 49), all potential 'dangerous conversations'.

FBV: The 'gathering in' of troublesome populations?

As discussed in Chapter Four, the majority of the teacher-respondents understood British values to be absorbed within the already existing practices of their schools, resulting in little that was new. As a result, they saw the promotion of FBV as relatively insignificant once the policy had seemingly become embedded in the everyday life of the institution. Their schools had avoided monocultural, exclusionary images of 'Britishness'; the only visible reminder might be a corridor poster listing the values, or an entry on the school website stating how the school promoted FBV. From all the case study schools, teachers who spoke of the policy as being more overtly useful to them were those at Moreton Grange Secondary Academy (predominantly White British working-class population) and Garden Primary (mixed class, predominantly British Asian and majority Muslim population). Both schools offer pertinent examples of the adaptation of the FBV agenda to (perceived) local circumstances. As policies shift across local landscapes, new possibilities and sensibilities are established, so policy is 'talked' and thought about and enacted differently (Ball, personal communication, 2018).

Staff at both schools felt that their student populations would benefit from increased exposure to liberal democratic principles. This raises complex issues of clashes between the liberal values that the teachers felt they were promoting and of the presumed 'otherness' of the students' families, which, for reasons of space, I can only begin to outline here. The rationale for promoting liberal values, especially when the 'problem' is located in the students' families, is not as straightforward as may first appear. Is the promotion of the FBV intended to offer students an alternative viewpoint to those assumed to be held by their families? To guide families? Or to discipline them?

At both Garden and Moreton Grange, staff perceived some of the parents to be intolerant. At Moreton Grange, respondents described prejudiced attitudes around race and religion from the students, parents and local community, which they saw as important for the school to challenge. At Garden Primary, John, the headteacher, had introduced a strong strand of work around identity, focusing on accepting difference and on promoting equalities of race, religion, sexuality, disability and gender as a form of defence against what he understood to be incursions by religiously conservative parents (he spoke of "hidden agendas" and "manipulation").

John, while describing home–school relationships as generally positive, related significant value clashes with parents, including a dispute with a Muslim community group, differences in views on girls wearing hijabs (which very few did), the parent–teacher association wanting to plan a women-only event, and parental suspicion of sex education. His tone was sometimes antagonistic:

'We would see things like challenging families for keeping children out of SRE as very much connected to that. The suppression of feminist rights, that is something we are talking about with … Year Five and Six girls, there has been a strong backlash about letting girls – you know "I don't want my daughter to be in the SRE lesson", she is too young for that. "What? Do you think she is going to get pregnant?" Would you like her to be a dutiful little girl wearing a hijab, is that it, because you won't let your wife learn English?", and it is very oppressive, so we are kind of flying the flag for those children.'

Sex and relationships education (SRE)[8] is undoubtedly an issue of concern to many conservative religious parents, and staff at Newton Primary School had also found the issue difficult and controversial (the headteacher there responded through repeated dialogues with parents[9]). Such clashes are likely to be experienced by school staff as painful, personal and exhausting. However, John's attitude is one of alertness to, almost an expectation of, incursions. Referring to attempts by a mosque and a synagogue (visited by children on school trips) to sit boys and girls separately, he comments:

'It is hard, you have to be principled about this. You need to be vigilant about all those nasty little things that are going on. … If we allow that to happen, we would be sending a message to the children that you can be discriminated against. I am standing up for your [the children's] rights even though you don't even know I am doing it and you haven't asked me to and the parents don't want it. But I am like the moral guardian. That is one of our roles, to be here and to protect people's rights and to be moral about things. It is very important ... There are cultural sensitivities, but you know you do live in England and we want to treat everybody the same. So, we can respect what you want to do as long as it fits in with our responsibility to protect children, that is what we are here for.'

Here again is the idea of the teacher as a moral agent, and again – but more forcefully this time – challenging perceived parental and community intolerance (also Don, Downs). John's "muscular liberalism" – Charles Taylor's (1994) 'liberalism as a fighting creed' (cited in Meer, 2010: 52) – positions him, the staff and the school's curriculum as a bulwark, shielding the children, against their parents, community and religion. This is, I argue, symptomatic of a general political and social climate that is hyper-vigilant of the possibility of illiberal actions from Muslim populations (see also Holmwood and O'Toole, 2018) – John refers to the Trojan Horse affair. This 'surplus of meaning', whereby religious identification is presumed to be the explanation for all the actions and the comportment of those identified as Muslim (Wesselhoeft, 2017) is an example of the affective policy 'tone' emanating from the contemporary structure of feeling (see Chapter Three). John offered strong support of liberal democratic values but also few signs of accommodation with the (assumed) culture of some of the pupils' families, understanding them to be isolated from the (White) mainstream and noting that "There is almost no White population here. It was much more helpful when we were mixed". He does not appear to hold a pluralistic conception of citizenship, a key aspect of which Ajani describes as 'regarding the stranger as having equal dignity and moral worth' (2015: 137).

Teachers at the other schools in the research with large Muslim populations generally maintained a less critical and conflictual stance in relation to the families of their students, and acknowledged the discrimination faced by Muslim communities, as these examples show:

'People are wary because when you talk about Prevent actually to people's mindset what that is about is making sure that you don't have Muslim extremism. … It kind of says that although actually it means any right-wing groups but no, it is not what people have in their mindset. It is not what people do … I think even the term itself, Prevent, that is for every student in this school, that is what it means, it means it is talking about them.' (Grishma, senior leader, *East Heath Secondary*)

[After 9/11 and 7/7 the local Bangladeshi-heritage community] 'felt very much under attack – because they were.' (Margaret, headteacher, *Albernay Secondary*)

[In a discussion after the 2017 London Bridge terror attack] 'I really noticed in my Y7 class, three [Muslim] girls … normally they are very vocal. They just turned off and I can see in their faces that it was intimidating.' (Azar, teacher, *Point High Academy*)

'Even [Muslim] members of staff … their families … say, "Just be really careful, you don't want to be seen as someone who might cause a problem." So, the best thing is just to be silent.' (Alesandro, teacher, Holy Church Secondary)

The other population 'diagnosed' by teachers as in particular 'need' of 'British values', especially mutual respect and tolerance, were the White British working classes (see also Osler 2011). My data are limited here but teachers at Valley High and *Point High*, both multiethnic schools with significant White British middle-class populations, saw little problem with racism or xenophobia; students were understood to have generally respectful and appreciative attitudes towards ethnic and religious diversity:

> 'What I was saying before about what our concerns are, it doesn't seem to be racism, there is this gender thing which is deeply worrying [some boys' sexualised behaviour towards girls] … But I think the kids here are very, very attuned to the comments of racism and I think they put religious stuff into that container. So, they will be shocked if they heard anybody, not that it never happens, but you know just in the same way as if anybody used the N-word there would be gasps of "Oh my God!" And I think that is very widespread in the school.' (Dominic, Valley High, mixed class, multiethnic population; see also Bennett and Lee-Treeweek, 2014)

> '[The students] are predominantly liberal here.' (Azar, *Point High*, mixed class, multiethnic population)

There was some disquiet voiced by teachers at Downs Secondary (rural/suburban area, majority White British population, mixed social class) over students' attraction to UKIP's arguments on immigration. However, among the case study schools, it was particularly at Moreton Grange, with a mainly White British working-class population, where attitudes concerning race and religion were of particular concern to teachers. Their aim was to broaden the outlook of young people who, it was felt, were living in a homogeneous and inward-looking town, and in particular to raise their participation rates in higher education. As discussed earlier, a study of terrorism was introduced into RE for the younger teenagers (11–14 years) specifically to address what was understood to be the students' tendency to xenophobia:

> 'When I was teaching RE, I had to teach a topic on terrorism [to Year 7, 11–12-year-olds] and … this still baffles me, I had to explain the difference between a terrorist and an asylum–seeker, an illegal immigrant, an immigrant, and a refugee, and they thought that they all meant the same thing. And that was really quite shocking to me. Don't get me wrong, my family is also from [town] and I'm not immune to the fact that people have prejudices but it was quite shocking to think that that is genuinely what they thought.' (Agnes, Moreton Grange Secondary Academy, urban area, White British, predominantly working–class population)

Teachers at Moreton Grange thus prioritised challenging prejudice on the grounds of race or religion. They described the local White British population as "insular". It is beyond the scope of the data to comment on parental attitudes to diversity, or on how such attitudes may be shaped by place and its intersection with social class. It is interesting, however, to consider Walkerdine and Jimenez's (2012) study of the affective experience of being part of an economically deprived, close-knit area in their research in 'Steeltown'. They explore the economic underpinning of insularity, arguing that the solidarity developed among residents in relation to economic uncertainty (the future of the steel industry) also held 'townspeople in a rigid containment' with 'a strict sense of rules about conduct, a resistance to outsiders and the inability of people to leave the town' (2012: 55). Moreton Grange is also located in a town that suffered from the collapse of traditional manufacturing industries. This suggests that the agenda of the teachers, which stressed both tolerance of and respect for difference, and individual aspiration (in the form of going to university), may be coming from a different affective place and perspective from the outlook of some of the local working-class families. Haylett argues further that the assumption of discriminatory attitudes among the White working classes allows the middle classes to present themselves, in contrast, as modern, liberal and cosmopolitan:

> The white working-class 'other' [is] emblematically a throwback ... This middle-class dependency on working-class 'backwardness' for its own claim to modern multicultural citizenship is an unspoken interest within the discourse of illegitimacy around the white working-class poor. (Haylett, 2001: 365)

She continues that what goes unspoken in all of this is the economic inequalities that 'arise from a dominant class-based anglo-centrism whose power is manifest in its ability to remain unnamed and respectably normal' (2001: 366). Indeed, it was notable that in the work all the case study schools did on equality issues, social class inequalities in England rarely appeared (although global inequalities were more frequently discussed, for example via the fair trade campaign). Social class largely appears to exist outside the 'domain of the sayable' and where class impacts upon school processes (e.g. in Moreton Grange's attempts to encourage more students to go to university) it does so at the level of students working on themselves to raise their aspirations.

The curriculum initiatives at Garden and Moreton Grange were, as in the earlier examples in Chapter Four, developed by individual teachers who invested a considerable amount of time, expertise and labour in response to what they understood to be students' 'needs', in line with their understanding of their role as moral agents and their desire to educate their students to have "good morals, ethics" (Rich, Garden Primary, cited earlier). Teachers at both schools seek to promote liberal values to children against their apparently illiberal families, but this is not a simple or unproblematic mission. There are three points here: one is that, arguably, some specific examples of individual prejudice from parents or students come to speak, in teachers' understandings, for entire local communities. Second, the promotion of liberal values can tip over into the disciplining of parents by schools, a position that leaves little room for dialogue. Both can result in a sense of embattlement and antagonism, as seems to be the case at Garden. Finally, the attribution of prejudice and intolerance appears to cohere around Muslim bodies and White British working-class bodies, leaving the White middle-class body as without blame (although not completely, as in the case of Valley High, where boys' attitudes towards girls are perceived as exploitative). John at Garden asserted that staff there are "flying the flag for children" and, while this is not a reference to British values per se, it does describe a process of 'gathering in' to modernist liberal values those ethnic, racial and classed 'others' who are understood to be 'saturated' (Fortier 2008: 35) by their pre-modern values.

Conclusion

In this chapter, I have discussed three main issues. The first is teachers' promotion of mutual respect and tolerance. In their conversations with me, these were the FBV on which teachers focused their attention. I have suggested that the promotion of these particular values was a professional priority, enacted by these teachers independently of and well before the FBV mandate. Further, I argued that this prioritising of the development of students as good moral beings does affective 'work' in allowing teachers to maintain a 'thick' professionalism, fuller and more complete than one that focuses solely on meeting performance targets. This does not mean that the teacher-respondents are necessarily positioning themselves as *against* a performative culture. Rather, they are insisting on a moral dimension as necessary to complete their role within that culture.

Next, I moved on to discuss how the teachers engaged with controversial/sensitive issues. I identified the practical and affective challenges and constraints on their doing so, and also indicated the possibilities of 'dangerous conversations'. Third, I detailed how FBV were understood in some schools to have a role in inculcating liberal values and domesticating difference within a framework of national unity (Haylett, 2001). While some differences are to be welcomed, others are understood to be inherently cultural and generally 'backward' (Kofman, 2005), or at least in need of modernising, and still others (of social class) are rarely mentioned explicitly in the classroom.

Thus, teachers in this research emphasised a generally worded but strongly held belief in encouraging an attitude of equality of respect among students, as one that should guide young people's behaviour as a current school citizen and also as a future adult citizen. They managed to maintain, and indeed some strengthened, this approach in the face of the growing instances of lack of respect and tolerance that they identified in relation to politics and the wider society in England and abroad. This approach did have some limitations, however. Teachers were trying to build solidarity and communality in their schools. As the headteacher of Shire Primary School said: "for me it is about embedding that understanding that we are all different and we are all the same and we are all one community." There are three caveats here. The first is that the mantra of ' "Equal but different" ignores and obscures the power relations inherent in different ethnicities and cultures' (Bennett and Lee-Treeweek 2014: 36); not being White British (especially in a majority White British school like Shire) is still a departure from the 'norm'. The second caveat is that the teachers' messages of respect and tolerance may be rather weakly articulated in relation to the driving force of their institutions: the requirement to fulfil the performative project of achieving targets, leading them to focus on students as units of (variable degrees of) production. The third caveat is that the boundaries what seems 'sayable' and 'thinkable' in school acts to limit coverage of contemporary controversies, leaving children and young people with a disconnect between, on the one hand, the assertions of their teachers as to what their school and their state believes in terms of equality of respect, and on the other, what they see around them, especially if they belong to a disadvantaged population. Sadia, the headteacher at *Talib*, a state-funded Muslim faith school, explicitly recognised this disconnect:

> 'And then this ... kid passed by [i.e. in the street] and [said] "Fuck Islam" and I said, "Kid do you even know what Islam is really?" Obviously, he wasn't in the least bothered and he walked off. In his mind he had victory where he had said something to this Muslim-looking woman and walked off. So, I wish really that the amount of effort we are taking here in Talib Primary School to teach our children that respect for others, others are doing the same thing. Because what I worry sometimes is that we almost drill in our children, "have respect for other people regardless of their backgrounds, regardless of how much you disagree with those people", but we know the reality is very different. When they step out of the school, they face discrimination first hand and [this multiethnic urban area] is one of the areas which you know, high poverty, and ... the trust in government is not incredibly strong in these communities. Muslims are not the only ones having this problem.'

Thus, the range of legitimate citizen identities offered by teachers to children and young people, both as present-day citizens of the school and as future adult citizens of the nation, have many positives in the modelling and promulgating of an equality of respect. The limited focus (although for very understandable reasons) on contemporary political and social issues, however, leaves biases and absences unspoken and often unrecognised, and thus the present distribution of power and inequality remains largely undisturbed.

Notes

1   I have put 'political' in inverted commas to signal the common understanding of 'political' as related to party politics and/or the processes of a national government. However, broader understandings of 'political' understand politics to be about the working out of power and that neutrality is also a political stance.

2   These letter grades have been superseded and GCSE national exams (taken at 16 years) now grade in numbers ranging from 1 to 9.

3   Regional Schools Commissioners hold academies accountable for their exam results.

4   Cantle's definition of 'dangerous conversations' differs somewhat from the common definitions of controversial issues, which are usually defined as issues on which there are differing positions based on alternative values (Stradling, 1985, cited in Oulton et al, 2004: 490). Cantle's definition is clearly focused on issues related to living within a diverse society and on moving young people away from prejudice towards 'others'.

5   I have adopted both practical and affective categories of explanation here in order to discuss the avoidance/limitation of 'dangerous conversations'. The affective category blurs the distinction between conscious and unconscious avoidance. In the former, teachers avoid placing themselves in risky situations that may generate discomfort for them. In the latter, these situations are 'unthinkable'; embarking on 'dangerous conversations' is not what a 'good' teacher would consider for a lesson. However, the data do not suggest a clear distinction between the two.

6   Italics are used to identify those schools that I visited just once.

7   Don earlier defined this as not overtly racist.

8   SRE has been renamed by the government "relationships and sex education" (RSE).

9   A current (at the time of writing, May 2019) example of a clash between the values of some conservative Muslim parents and a school is the dispute at Parkfield Community School in Birmingham, England. The 'No Outsiders' programme, which teaches children to respect difference in line with the Equality Act 2010, was used successfully by Andrew Moffatt at this school for a number of years and is widely acclaimed. However, in 2019, soon

after publicity on government plans to make RSE compulsory in English schools, protests against the programme's approach started and grew. There were complaints about some of the picturebooks in the large collection used with the children, which includes *Mommy, Mama and Me* (featuring a child and her lesbian parents engaged in everyday activities) and *King and King* (featuring a prince who marries a man). The protests were directed at what is perceived to be the promotion of LGBT+ lifestyles. They ran for two months, leaving the lessons suspended and staff feeling stressed and under attack. The school and others in the area are currently in discussion with parents, and the Secretary of State for Education has clarified that parents cannot exercise a veto on what schools teach.

SIX

Conclusion: citizenship, values and belonging

Even as we challenge dominant discourses and the specific language which feeds and sustains them, we may find ourselves doing so within those discourses' own frames of reference, constrained by the very language with which they seek to determine our thoughts, words, deeds. (Moore, 2018: 145–6)

[Both welfare professionals and those who work actively for equality and diversity] are all situated ambivalently, implicated in inequality's reproduction as well as its challenge. (Hunter, 2015: 144)

I finished the previous chapter by highlighting the ambivalent position – also illustrated by these quotations – of the teachers who invest considerable time, energy and commitment in highlighting and explicitly promoting respect and tolerance to students, (other FBV have a much lower profile, as discussed). As the 'good' professional cannot be an 'unreasonable' one, teachers' promotion works through a discourse of liberal 'reasonableness' (Chetty, 2018) that fails to recognise the entanglement of long-standing classed and raced inequalities in defining what 'we' know and should transmit through education. This absence of acknowledgement produces a curriculum and pedagogy that 'suggest[s] not moving too far from where we are and not looking too closely at how we got here' (Chetty, 2018: 9), a stance that also has to overlook the determining role of current high-stakes testing in shaping what are understood to be 'effective' curricula and pedagogies. Given this situation, there are 'no straightforwardly heroic, noble acts of resistance' (Hunter, 2015: 144). However, in this chapter, I go on to briefly consider whether particular approaches to citizenship education have the potential to offer considerations of liberal democratic values that go beyond the simplistic, assumed consensus of FBV. But, first, I shall summarise my arguments to this point.

The enactment of FBV

Ball, Maguire and Braun identify a major tension visible in recent education policy as being that between 'neo-conservative and neo-liberal versions of government, knowledge and social authority' (2012: 140). The FBV policy, however, exemplifies both. The influence of neoconservatism is visible in the idea of promoting a set of national values. This raises questions about equal belonging to the polity, and the likelihood of the effectiveness of a policy that seeks to enforce uniform commitments and loyalties on everyone, despite unequal starting points in terms of whether people perceive themselves, and others perceive them, as full citizens. The influence of neoliberalism is visible in the way in which values education does not focus on the political principles of FBV, but rather looks 'inward' rather than 'outward' (encouraging working on oneself). This is a neoliberal enterprise (Sant et al, 2018: 83) operating within a system that emphasises measurable performance targets and allows limited opportunities for critical education about citizenship.

In this book, I have argued that understanding the context of the enactment of any policy is vital if the workings out of the policy on the ground are to be fully understood. I have suggested that there are two major sets of contextual influences to be considered with regard to the requirement to promote FBV. The first is the trend in the political and social climate towards populism and authoritarianism that coalesces in narrow interpretations of nationality and nationhood. This is shaped by the anxiety, and sometimes hostility, shown by governments across Europe about the integration of 'others', especially Muslim 'others', both newcomers and those born here; the current furore around the UK leaving the European Union; and the increasing polarisation of societal attitudes in relation to nation, difference and cohesion (as seen in the UK, Germany, Brazil and the US, among others, with the rise of the far right).[1] How teachers respond to the FBV, a policy apparently intended to strengthen national identity and belonging, is also influenced by the affective policy tone, the 'structure of feeling', of living in a particular political and social moment (Chapter Three). Given this, I have detailed teacher–respondents' efforts to work against the prevailing climate of intolerance.

The second set of influences revolves around the role played by externally imposed forms of accountability in schools. These measures call into being particular behaviours from teachers if they are to be compliant (Chapter Five). The demands of accountability also result in the marginalisation of non-examined activity, such as discussion of contemporary political and social issues, thereby side-lining obvious 'homes' for these discussions: the non-EBacc subjects of PSHE, RE and citizenship education (Chapters One and Three).

Following the literature on policy enactment, I have emphasised (Chapter Three) that policies, especially ones as generally worded as the FBV requirement, are not implemented in any straightforward manner on the ground, and that teachers have considerable room for translating policies to fit with what they perceive to be the 'needs' of their students and the practicalities of having to respond to this and myriad other demands. Thus, minimalist responses, such as putting up posters listing the FBV, may be seen as a rational and efficient way of addressing the requirement to promote the values. In Chapter Four, I identified four main responses to FBV found in this study. Elements of these overlap in some sites, and particular individual responses are nuanced by teachers' individual beliefs and histories and the micro-contexts in which they find themselves. There is more to say about these nuances than can be contained in a book of this length, so I have focused here on the broader commonalities and differences between teachers' responses. The four approaches are *Representing Britain*, *Repackaging* and *Relocating* the FBVs, and *Engagement* with them.

Drawing on the nationalism literature, I argued in Chapter Two that the traditional positioning of civic and ethnic nationalism as dichotomous overlooks the way in which, in practice, civic nationalism (belonging based on commitment to political principles such as the FBV) may be permeated by ethnic nationalism (belonging based on shared ethnicity or heritage). This permeation was illustrated in Chapter Two in the approach I have called *Representing Britain*, an approach that proceeds from and promotes 'Britishness' as closed and unchanging. Here are instances of everyday nationalism, that is, taken-for-granted representations of nationhood. It seems that the teachers who responded to the FBV requirement by planning visual representations of 'Britishness' reached for images representing a united, and mostly White, Britain, emphasising tradition and heritage through cosy images of an imaginary past, present and future. Since the 2016 EU referendum, such images of Britain, harking back to an imagined past, have been part of the debate about the nation's future outside the EU, a 'last gasp of the old empire', as Dorling and Tomlinson (2019) put it.

Representing Britain was not the majority response of teachers in my study, however. This was *Repackaging*, which describes schools absorbing the promotion of FBV into their current practices. This minimises the policy's demands upon staff and students, and avoids exclusionary imagery, but it does not develop any of the opportunities that the policy requirement appears to open up, or encourage the giving of more time to exploring issues of belonging, citizenship and nationhood. I also discussed the limitations of school council meetings as a lived example of democracy, despite their common repackaging as fulfilling the requirement to promote that FBV.

Relocating the values is a related response to *Repackaging*. It describes the promotion of FBV as subsumed within other work on values. When values are the focus for explicit teaching, I argue that this is likely to be in the form of inward-directed character education rather than outward-directed citizenship education, the former focusing on individual emotional and moral development, with 'performance virtues' (e.g. perseverance, excellence, resilience) seeming to dominate in many sites.

However, I also note the conviction of the teacher-respondents that their role included modelling, and in particular explicitly teaching virtuous behaviour in relation to others. Indeed, the FBV that teachers discussed most was the promotion of mutual respect and tolerance, noting that "we were doing this anyway". Although what this promotion meant in practice was often rather generally expressed, there was nevertheless a clear commitment to disseminating a message of equal respect to inform how students treat each other within the school community, and also as an attitude to take forward into adult life. I have tried to explore the affective elements of citizenship – how students are taught to feel about themselves and others – and in this respect the case study schools presented a consistent view of 'good' citizenship for their students. For students, as present-day citizens of the school, 'good' citizenship is about respecting all within the institution and developing the performance virtues needed to succeed and conform in adult life. Additionally, there were also occasional initiatives around active citizenship (fundraising, letter writing, engagements with the surrounding community, e.g. Kenton's regular teas with senior citizens). In a few cases, individuals spoke explicitly of wishing to develop students' sense of themselves as having an autonomous and assertive voice (e.g. Valley High's and Downs' headteachers: see Chapter Five).

Fully understanding teachers' shared focus on equal respect and tolerance presents several issues. Given the particular context of growing concerns about intolerance, rising levels of hate crime and the frequent assumption by politicians that difference is a threat (Chapter 1), then, arguably, such work by teachers is hugely valuable. I started this book citing Honig's (2001) notion of 'our' ambivalence towards 'the foreigner' (including those born in the nation but still positioned as 'foreign'), with xenophobia and xenophilia coexisting uneasily, although surely with a tilt towards xenophobia in the political climate since Honig was writing. Yet the response of teacher-respondents has largely tilted the other way, towards xenophilia. This is especially the case for most teachers in the multiethnic case study schools, who seek to celebrate diversity, and to promote the idea of difference as enriching rather than a threat or source of anxiety and of Britain as a multiracial society comfortable with itself. However, I have also sought to emphasise that this is far from an unproblematic positioning, limited and constrained in various ways.

I have argued that the generality of the teachers' responses, their role as institutional actors in dividing and classifying students, and the apparent limitations on what can be said and taught in schools if the teacher is still to remain 'professional' and in control all act to call into question the impact on students of teachers' attempts to teach 'not [only] what it means for an individual to live well, but what she owes to others' (Clayton et al, 2018: 30). Furthermore, Zembylas (2014) argues that commonly cited teaching goals encouraging openness to and tolerance of difference – what he refers to as 'coping with difference' and 'embracing the other' – have to be critically interrogated for underlying emotional tensions and ambivalences. As an example, he offers the commonly expressed notion (cited in Chapter Five) that 'we are all different, we are all the same'. The 'other' is embraced as different but, as Zembylas (drawing on Fortier's work) asks, what and whose differences disappear to make us all the same? Differentiation persists between the normal and unmarked, and the non-normal – who should still be tolerated (Bowie, 2018: 208; Sant and Valencia, 2018). Despite their genuine commitment, most of the teacher–respondents did not have the scope or the space to look beneath and around their exhortations of respect and tolerance. Thus, the existing power relations in and outside schools remain largely unquestioned.

As cited in Chapter Five, Moore and Clarke describe teaching as a 'fantasy of equality of opportunity' (2016: 670). Teachers seek to fulfil their professional aims for the *all-round* development of *all* young people despite their unequal starting points; the institutionalised processes which place barriers in the way of the desired development for some young people (resulting, for example, in the low level of educational qualifications gained by children excluded from mainstream schools); and the wider social, economic and political context which see 'fantasies … fraying, includ[ing], particularly, upward mobility, job security, political and social equality' (Berlant, 2011: 3).

Arguably, another fantasy is the discourse of 'reasonableness' in relation to teaching respect and tolerance and other values. Throughout the book, I have been commenting on the way in which citizenship education in many English schools has been reduced in status in recent years, but, as I started to outline in Chapter Five, there are more fundamental difficulties with a strategy of *Engagement* (my fourth response), concerning the conceptualisation of the aims of citizenship education, its appropriate content and how it should be taught in schools.

The implicit framing of the subject suggests that 'more' and 'better' citizenship education requires identifying the correct and appropriate body of knowledge and arguments to be conveyed through the correct pedagogy, and that this *will* result in tolerant and respectful attitudes in the students. Similarly, Strandbrink (2017) argues that the implicit promise of saturating young people with particular liberal democratic values of tolerance, cosmopolitanism and universalism is unlikely to be realised, partly because civic/citizenship education commonly depends on a 'soft', cosmopolitan (Goren and Yemini, 2017), and instrumentalist/technicist approach (Strandbrink, 2017; see also Biesta and Lawey, 2006). Moreover, Strandbrink claims that liberal democratic values are often presented as having a coherence and agreed definition that they actually lack, and that they are implicitly presented as European values to civilise non-Europeans, overlooking Europe's 'shadowy legacy of bad values' (e.g. imperialism, anti-Semitism, racism, fascism: Strandbrink, 2017: 74; see also Kiwan, 2018). On this basis, Strandbrink argues that students will have to 'struggle in order to assemble meaningful comprehensive worldview packages' (p. 172) from rather vague and often non-committal subject matter that may not address their immediate concerns, as I argued at the end of Chapter Five.

However, from the point of view of practising teachers, such arguments must appear to suggest that their efforts lack any meaning or validity. Strandbrink ends his discussion of civics/citizenship education by highlighting its fallibility, but observes that comprehensive programmes to educate young people in liberal democratic values are 'really the worst form of civic enculturation imaginable – except that is for all other forms' (2017: 206). So, with this in mind, I shall briefly review an approach to citizenship education that does begin to address at least some of the complexities around citizenship, belonging and nationhood.

Global citizenship education and human rights

Commentators have argued that, in the light of technological developments, the global movement of capital and increased migration flows, there has been a growing understanding of the need for educators to move beyond traditional ideas of citizenship education as aiming to build a common national identity. This has led to the development of broader conceptualisations of citizenship inherent in global citizenship education that place human rights at the centre 'since all students, regardless of their nationality and migration status, are holders of human rights' (Osler and Starkey 2018: 34–5; Yemini et al 2018; Farrell 2019).

However, GCE is not easily defined (Oxley and Morris, 2013). It is indeed a 'moving montage' (Gaudelli, 2009: 82, cited in Goren and Yemini, 2017: 171). In a recent textbook, Sant and colleagues (2018) include discussions on varied topics placed under the heading of GCE – citizenship, social justice, education for diversity, development education, character education, peace education and sustainable development education. They note the similarities and differences across these dimensions and ask whether this complexity is evidence of intellectual dynamism or simply incoherence (Sant et al, 2018: 8). As indicated in Chapter Two, discussions around GCE also suggest that the label has and is applied to different forms with different outcomes: from an investment in the neoliberal self, developing the attitudes and knowledge that young people need to compete effectively in the global market place, what Dill calls 'global competencies' (2013, cited in Goren and Yemini, 2017: 171; see also Pais and Costa, 2017), to engaging with the roots of inequalities, whether local or global – Dill's 'global consciousness' which aims to develop a 'global orientation' (2013, cited in Goren and Yemini, 2017: 171). The latter requires centring 'the complex relations of power at the heart of what it means to relate to other citizens' (Sant et al, 2017), and may be referred to as 'critical' (Andreotti 2006) or 'transformative' (Bamber et al, 2018a) citizenship education, although there are other variations (for a review see Sant et al, 2018).

Commentators on critical citizenship education suggest a number of areas – issues of pedagogy, curricula and school organisation – which could offer opportunities for critically engaging with the liberal democratic values of the FBV. The word 'critical' is often vaguely defined, and as a result heavily overused (Johnson and Morris, 2010). Johnson and Morris nevertheless defend 'critical pedagogy', an approach that draws on Freire's work, focusing on affect, in order to reveal inequalities and encouraging students to consider what action would improve the status quo. Similar ground is covered by Osler and Starkey in their threefold understanding of rights:

> As well as knowledge (learning about rights), there is an emphasis on learning through rights (democratic upbringing and school practices, such as student councils and a climate that promotes recognition and respect of difference). Finally, there is learning for rights. This involves empowering young people to be able to make a difference, and equipping them with skills for change. It involves seeing human rights education as a means of transformation. (2018: 37)

In critical framings of GCE, empathy for others is (mostly) held as crucial but insufficient (Andreotti et al, 2015), if it remains what Zembylas calls a 'sentimental discourse of suffering' (2013b: 505). To avoid this, he writes of encouraging students to engage in small-scale compassionate action (e.g. letter writing, volunteering for non-governmental organisations). Writers also suggest an emphasis on open-ended pedagogic processes which involve students in what is to be taught, and which are not framed around a search for the 'right' answer (Bamber et al, 2018b). Relatedly, Sant et al (2017; see also

Sant and González-Valencia, 2018) discuss the generation of agonistic spaces (drawing on the writing of Chantal Mouffe), foregrounding a recognition that conflicting views on controversial issues are inevitable, and that consensus may not be possible or possible only on fragile, temporary grounds.

Alternative curricula and pedagogic approaches cannot be easily inserted into an existing education system, and even if this occurs in part, such approaches are unequal to challenging existing discursive formations of the purposes of schooling, and the current constructions of the 'good' teacher and the 'good' education. However, a planned and progressive programme of citizenship education could, at least, move beyond the blunt generalisations of the FBV policy to offer and debate with students the worth of an identity as 'citizens of a pluralistic society' (QCA, 2004, cited in Quartermaine, 2016: 23), and to recognise and encourage their identifications with the multiple communities to which they belong (Starkey, 2018). I suggest that this starts with those contemporary political and social issues that relate to living with diversity and 'the actual conditions of young people's citizenship' (Biesta and Lawey, 2006: 74). Chapter Five includes some topics identified by teacher-respondents, but different issues may be identified by students as relevant to them at different times and in different localities.

Last word

Debates about diversity and cohesion will doubtless persist as global population mobilities continue. I have focused here on one policy reaction to diversity. The requirement to promote FBV derived from a state-led concern over a minority extremist threat to the majority, and engaged with and built on White British ethnic nationalist inclinations to identify as an imperative, the further integration of ethnic minorities, especially Muslims, into the liberal polity.

The promotion of fundamental British values as currently enacted is distant from the more progressive developments of global citizenship education. It posits the development of commonly held values that can help young people, regardless of ethnicity, class, religion and so on, to live together based on a shared attachment to these political and social principles, values that are asserted as universally applicable. What I have tried to show through this study is that, despite the apparent promise of national belonging for all who commit to these values, narrow and exclusive definitions persist of who truly belongs and is able to fit in, who confidently inhabits and is understood to inhabit these values. The particular format and enactments of the FBV requirement do not encourage the degree of critical deliberation that might ensure that ideas of nationality and nationhood are not fixed and closed, but fluid and open to redetermination as the population profile develops (Bamber et al, 2018b: 435). Nor does FBV currently provide the basis for an in-depth examination of how we as a society perceive diversity and cohesion and the possibilities and limitations of our current understandings. The requirement to promote FBV was seemingly aimed at challenging extremist thought, but is unlikely to be effective in this, given the lack of detailed definitions of either 'extremism', 'radicalisation' or students' 'resilience' to these phenomena (Crawford et al, 2018). As discussed in Chapter Five in relation to Garden Primary School, the FBV requirement may be used to promote liberal values, at times in an illiberal manner, shutting down the possibility of dialogue with families and making assumptions influenced by families' faith and/or class-based identities of their opposition to liberal democratic values. Nor is the FBV requirement an effective way to establish areas of consensus and commonality in a diverse society, because, as this research illustrates, it did not lead to the sorts of discussions and debates which could allow children and young people to voice their perceptions of relationships in their local areas, what the fault-lines and divisions, and the commonalities and points of solidarity, are and could be.

Finally, the requirement to promote FBV was not, in this research, an inspiring approach to educating young people about citizenship, as its explicit promotion largely consisted of posters, arrays of Union Jacks, and reruns of discussions about toilets, food and mobile phones in school council meetings badged as promoting democracy. Developing students' understanding of and commitment to any set of political and social values must surely require exploration and debate around their meaning and their practice in our society. This could be enabled by a programme of critical citizenship education, notwithstanding its limitations. As it is, the FBV are likely to remain at best merely words and pictures on a school display board, and at worst words and pictures that actively work to exclude.

Note

[1] The rise of the far right in Britain was reported on by the Lead Commissioner for Countering Extremism, Sara Khan, to the Parliamentary Home Affairs Committee in October 2018.

References

Abbott, L. and Clarke, S. (2016) *OCR Religious Studies GCSE*. London: Hodder.

Adams, R. (2018) Government accused of covering up schools' cuts with misleading figures. *The Guardian*, 4 October.

Ahmed, S. (2014) *The Cultural Politics of Emotion* (2nd edn). Edinburgh: Edinburgh University Press.

Ajani, M. (2015) *Citizenship, the Self and the Other.* Cambridge: Cambridge Scholars Publishing.

Allen, C. (2010) *Islamophobia*. London: Routledge.

Anderson, Ben (2016) Neoliberal affects. *Progress in Human Geography*, 40(6): 734–53.

Anderson, Benedict (2006) *Imagined Communities*. London: Verso.

Anderson, Bridget (2016) Against fantasy citizenship: the politics of migration and austerity. *Renewal: A Journal of Labour Politics*, 24(1): 53–62.

Andreotti, V. (2006) *Soft versus Critical Global Citizenship Education in Development Education: Policy and Practice*. Centre for the Study of Social and Global Justice, Nottingham University.

Andreotti, V., Biesta, G. and Ahenakew, C. (2015) Between the nation and the globe: education for global mindedness in Finland. *Globalisation, Societies and Education*, 13(2): 246–59.

Antonsich, M. (2016) International migration and the rise of the 'civil' nation. *Journal of Ethnic and Migration Studies*, 42(11): 1790–807.

Antonsich, M. and Skey, M. (2017) Introduction: The persistence of banal nationalism, in M. Skey and M. Antonsich (eds) *Everyday Nationhood*. London: Palgrave Macmillan.

Archer, L. and Francis, B. (2006) *Understanding Minority Ethnic Achievement: Race, Gender, Class and 'Success'*. London: Routledge.

Arthur, J. (2015) Extremism and neo-liberal education policy: a contextual critique of the Trojan Horse affair in Birmingham schools. *British Journal of Educational Studies*, 63(3): 311–28.

Awan, I. (2018) 'I never did anything wrong' – Trojan Horse: a qualitative study uncovering the impact in Birmingham. *British Journal of Sociology of Education*, 39(2): 197–211.

Ball, S.J. (1993) What is policy? Texts, trajectories and toolboxes. *The Australian Journal of Education Studies*, 13(2): 10–17.

Ball, S.J. (1994) *Education Reform*. Milton Keynes: Open University Press.

Ball, S.J. (1997) Policy sociology and critical social research. *British Educational Research Journal*, 23(3): 257–74.

Ball, S.J. (2017) *The Education Debate* (3rd edn). Bristol: Policy Press.

Ball, S.J., Maguire, M. and Braun, A. (2012) *How Schools Do Policy: Policy Enactments in Secondary Schools*. London: Routledge.

Bamber, P., Lewin, D. and White, M. (2018a) (Dis-)Locating the transformative dimension of global citizenship education. *Journal of Curriculum Studies*, 50(2): 204–30.

Bamber, P., Bullivant, A., Clark, A. and Lundie, D. (2018b) Educating global Britain: perils and possibilities promoting 'national' values through critical global citizenship education. *British Journal of Educational Studies*, 66(4): 433–53.

Banks, J. (2014) Diversity, group identity, and citizenship education in a global age. *Journal of Education*, 194(3): 1–12.

Banks, J.A. (2017) Failed citizenship and transformative civic education. *Educational Researcher*, 46(7): 366–77.

Banting, K. and Kymlicka, W. (2017) (eds.) *The Strains of Commitment: The Political Sources of Solidarity in Diverse Societies*. Oxford: Oxford University Press.

Bari, M. (2012) London 2012: A celebration of Britain's diversity. Available at https://www.huffingtonpost.co.uk/muhammad-abdul-bari/olympics-london-2012-a-celebration_b_1292015.html [Accessed 9 May 2019].

Barker, M. (1981) *The New Racism: Conservatives and the Ideology of the Tribe*. London: Junction Books.

Bayley, C. (1989) *Imperial Meridian: The British Empire and the World, 1780–1830*. London: Routledge.

Bennett, J. and Lee-Treweek, G. (2014) Doing race: How secondary school pupils in mainly White schools construct 'race'. *Power and Education*, 6(1): 32–45.

Berlant, L. (2001) Trauma and ineloquence. *Journal for Cultural Research*, 5, 1: 41–58.

Berlant, L. (2011) *Cruel Optimism*. Durham, NC: Duke University Press.

Biesta, G. and Lawy, R. (2006) From teaching citizenship to learning democracy: overcoming individualism in research, policy and practice. *Cambridge Journal of Education*, 36(1): 63–79.

Billig, M. (1992) *Talking of the Royal Family*. London: Routledge.

Billig, M. (1995) *Banal Nationalism*. London: Sage.

Billig, M. (2017) Banal nationalism and the imagining of politics, in M. Skey and M. Antonsich (eds) *Everyday Nationhood: Theorising Culture, Identity and Belonging after Banal Nationalism*, London: Palgrave Macmillan, pp. 307–21.

Billig, M., Downey, J., Richardson, J., Deacon, D. and Golding, P. (2005) *'Britishness' in the last three general elections: from ethnic to civic nationalism: Report for the Commission for Racial Equality*. Loughborough: Loughborough University.

Boler, M. (1999) *Feeling Power: Emotions and Education*. New York: Routledge.

Bowie, R. (2018) Tolerance, its moral ambiguity and civic value for schools, in F. Panjwani, L. Revell, R. Gholami and M. Diboll (eds.) *Education and Extremisms*, London: Routledge, pp. 204–16.

Bradbury, A. (2013) From model minorities to disposable models: the de-legitimisation of educational success through discourses of authenticity. *Discourse: Studies in the Cultural Politics of Education*, 34(4): 548–61.

Bradbury, A. and Roberts-Holmes, G. (2017) *The Datafication of Primary and Early Years Education: Playing with Numbers*. London: Routledge.

Braun, A. and Maguire, M. (2018) Doing without believing: enacting policy in the English primary school. *Critical Studies in Education*, Online first: 1–15.

Braun, A., Maguire, M. and Ball, S.J. (2010) Policy enactments in the UK secondary school: examining policy, practice and school positioning. *Journal of Education Policy*, 25(4): 547–60.

Braun, A., Ball, S., Maguire, M. and Hoskins, K. (2011) Taking context seriously: towards explaining policy enactments in the secondary school. *Discourse: Studies in the Cultural Politics of Education*, 32(4): 585–96.

Bryan, H. (2017) Developing the political citizen: how teachers are navigating the statutory demands of the Counter-Terrorism and Security Act 2015 and the Prevent duty. *Education, Citizenship and Social Justice*, 12(3): 213–26.

Bulmer, M. and Solomos, J. (eds) (2017) *Multiculturalism, Social Cohesion and Immigration: Shifting Conceptions in the UK*. London: Routledge.

Busher, J., Choudhury, T., Thomas, P. and Harris, G. (2017) *What the Prevent Duty Means for Schools and Colleges in England: An Analysis of Educationalists' Experiences*. Aziz Foundation. Available at http:// azizfoundation.org.uk/wp-content/uploads/2017/07/What-the-Prevent-Duty-means-for-schools-and-colleges-in-England.pdf [Accessed 29 April 2019].

Butler, J. (1997) *Excitable Speech: A Politics of the Performative*. London: Routledge.

Byrne, B. (2017) Testing times: the place of the Citizenship Test in the UK immigration regime and new citizens' responses to it. *Sociology*, 51(2): 323–38.

Calhoun, C. (2017) The rhetoric of nationalism, in M. Skey and M. Antonsich (eds) *Everyday Nationhood: Theorising Culture, Identity and Belonging after Banal Nationalism*, London: Palgrave Macmillan, pp. 17–30.

Cameron, D. (2011) Speech on radicalisation and Islamic extremism. Munich, February 2011. Available at https://www.newstatesman.com/blogs/the-staggers/2011/02/terrorism-islam-ideology [Accessed 9 May 2019].

Cameron, D. (2014) British values aren't optional, they're vital. *Mail on Sunday*. June 14. Available at https://www.dailymail.co.uk/debate/article-2658171/DAVID-CAMERON-British-values-arent-optional-theyre-vital-Thats-I-promote-EVERY-school-As-row-rages-Trojan-Horse-takeover-classrooms-Prime-Minister-delivers-uncompromising-pledge.html [Accessed 9 May 2019].

Canovan, M. (1996) *Nationhood and Political Theory*. Cheltenham: Edward Elgar.

Cantle, T. (2001) *Community Cohesion: A Report of the Independent Review Team*. London: Home Office.

Cantle, T. (2015) It's time for dangerous conversations. *RE Today*, 33(1): 12–13.

Cantle, T. (2019) The birth of community cohesion. Available at http://tedcantle.co.uk/about-community-cohesion/ [Accessed 9 May 2019].

Chetty D. (2018) Racism as 'reasonableness': philosophy for children and the gated community of inquiry. *Ethics and Education*, 13(1): 39–54.

Clayton, M., Mason, A., Swift, A. and Wareham, R. (2018) *How to Regulate Faith Schools*. Impact 25. London: Wiley.

Closs Stephens, A. (2013) *The Persistence of Nationalism: From Imagined Communities to Urban Encounters*. London: Routledge.

Code, L. (2007) The power of ignorance, in S. Sullivan and N. Tuana (eds) *Race and Epistemologies of Ignorance*, New York: SUNY Press, pp. 213–29.

Colombo, E. (2015) Multiculturalisms: An overview of multicultural debates in western societies. *Current Sociology*, 63(6): 800–824.

Conversi, D. (2014) Between the hammer of globalization and the anvil of nationalism: is Europe's complex diversity under threat? *Ethnicities*, 14(1): 25–49.

Cotton, D. (2006) Teaching controversial environmental issues: neutrality and balance in the reality of the classroom, *Educational Research*, 48(2): 223–41.

Cowden, S. and Singh, G. (2017) Community cohesion, communitarianism and neoliberalism. *Critical Social Policy*, 37(2): 268–86.

Crawford, J., Ebner, J. and Hasan, U. (2018) The balanced nation, in F. Panjwani, L. Revell, R. Gholami, and M. Diboll (eds) *Education and Extremisms*, London: Routledge, pp. 146–59.

Curtis, B. (2002) Foucault on governmentality and population: The impossible discovery. *Canadian Journal of Sociology*, 27(4): 505–35.

Davies, I., Evans, M. and Reid, A. (2005) Globalising citizenship education? A critique of 'global education' and 'citizenship education'. *British Journal of Educational Studies*, 53(1): 66–89.

Davies, I., Ho, L.C., Kiwan, D., Peck, C.L., Peterson, A., Sant, E. and Waghid, Y. (eds) (2018) *The Palgrave Handbook of Global Citizenship and Education*, London: Palgrave Macmillan.

Davies, L. (2018) *Review of Educational Initiatives in Counter-Extremism Internationally: What Works?* The Segerstedt Institute, University of Gothenburg.

De Wilde, M. and Duyvendak, J. (2016) Engineering community spirit: the pre-figurative politics of affective citizenship in Dutch local governance. *Citizenship Studies*, 20(8): 973–93.

Dei, G. (2008) Anti-racism education for global citizenship. In M. Peters, A. Britton and H. Blee (eds), *Global Citizenship Education: Philosophy, Theory and Pedagogy*. Rotterdam: Sense.

Department for Education (DfE) (2013) *National Curriculum for England: Citizenship Programme of Study*. London: DfE. Available at https://www.gov.uk/government/publications/national-curriculum-in-england-citizenship-programmes-of-study [Accessed 9 May 2019].

Department for Education (DfE) (2014) *Promoting Fundamental British Values as Part of SMSC in Schools*. DFE-00679-2014. London: DfE.

Department for Education (DfE) (2018a) *Exploring Teacher Workload: Qualitative Research*. Research report. London: DfE/ CooperGibson Research.

Department for Education (DfE) (2018b) *Permanent and Fixed Period Exclusions in England 2016–17*. London: DfE.

Department of Immigration and Border Protection (2016) *Life in Australia: Australian Values and Principles*. Commonwealth of Australia. Available at https://immi.homeaffairs.gov.au/support-subsite/files/life-in-australia/lia_english_full.pdf [Accessed 9 May 2019].

Di Gregorio, M. and Merolli, J. (2016) Introduction: affective citizenship and the politics of identity, control, resistance. *Citizenship Studies*, 20(8): 933–42.

Dill, J. (2013) *The Longings and Limits of Global Citizenship Education: The Moral Pedagogy of Schooling in a Cosmopolitan Age*. London: Routledge.

Dorling, D. and Tomlinson, S. (2019) *Rule Britannia: Brexit and the End of the Empire*. London: Biteback Publishing.

Dunleavy, P. (1987) *Theories of the State: The Politics of Liberal Democracy*. London: Macmillan Education.

Ecclestone K. and Lewis L. (2014) Interventions for resilience in educational settings: challenging policy discourses of risk and vulnerability. *Journal of Education Policy*, 29(2): 195–216.

Edelman, M. J. (1964) *The symbolic uses of politics*. Urbana: University of Illinois Press.

Edyvane, D. (2011) Britishness, belonging and the ideology of conflict: lessons from the polis. *Journal of Philosophy of Education*, 45(1): 75–93.

Eliot, T.S. (1948) *Notes towards the Definition of Culture*. London: Faber & Faber.

Elliott, J. (1983) A curriculum for the study of human affairs: the contribution of Lawrence Stenhouse. *Journal of Curriculum Studies*, 15(2): 105–23.

Elton-Chalcraft, S., Lander, V., Revell, L., Warner, D. and Whitworth, L. (2017) To promote, or not to promote fundamental British values? Teachers' standards, diversity and teacher education. *British Educational Research Journal*, 43(1): 29–48.

Equality and Human Rights Commission (2014) *Public sector equality duty guidance for schools in England*. London: Equality and Human Rights Commission. Available at https://www.equalityhumanrights.com/sites/default/files/psed_guide_for_schools_in_england.pdf [Accessed 9 May 2019].

Etzioni, A. (1993) *The Spirit of Community*. New York: Touchstone.

Expert Subject Advisory Group (2015) *The Prevent Duty and Teaching Controversial Issues: Creating a Curriculum Response Through Citizenship*. London: Association of Citizenship Teachers.

Expert Subject Advisory Group for Citizenship (2017) *National Action Plan: Citizenship for All!* Available at https://www.teachingcitizenship.org.uk/sites/teachingcitizenship.org.uk/files/National%20Action%20Plan%20for%20Citizenship%205%20July%202017%20-%20final.pdf [Accessed 2 May 2018].

Farrell, F. (2019) 'Walking on egg shells': Brexit, British values and educational space. *Education and Training*, doi: 10.1108/ET-12-2018-0248.

Fortier, A.M. (2008) *Multicultural Horizons: Diversity and the Limits of the Civil Nation*. London: Routledge.

Fortier, A.M. (2010) Proximity by design? Affective citizenship and the management of unease. *Citizenship Studies*, 14(1): 17–30.

Fortier, A.M. (2016) Afterword: Acts of affective citizenship? Possibilities and limitations. *Citizenship Studies*, 20(8): 1038–44.

Fortier, A.M. (2017) The psychic life of policy: desire, anxiety and 'citizenisation' in Britain. *Critical Social Policy*, 37(1): 3–21.

Foster, A. (2018) The diversity of this royal wedding reveals a Britain far removed from 1981. Available at https://www.theguardian.com/uk-news/2018/may/19/the-diversity-of-this-royal-wedding-shows-how-far-we-have-come [Accessed 9 May 2019].

Foucault, M. (1982) The subject and power. *Critical Inquiry*, 8(4): 777–95.

Fozdar, F. and Low, M. (2015) 'They have to abide by our laws … and stuff': ethno-nationalism masquerading as civic nationalism. *Nations and Nationalism*, 21(3): 524–43.

Gagen, E. (2015) Governing emotions: Citizenship, neuroscience and the education of youth. *Transactions of the Institute of British Geographers*, 40(1): 140–52.

Gaudelli, W. (2009) Heuristics of global citizenship discourses towards curriculum enhancement. *Journal of Curriculum Theorizing*, 25(1): 68–85.

Gereluk, D. (2012) *Education, Extremism and Terrorism: What Should Be Taught in Citizenship Education and Why*. London: A & C Black.

Golder, B. (2007) Foucault and the genealogy of pastoral power. *Radical Philosophy Review*, 10(2): 157–76.

Goode, J. (2018) Everyday patriotism and ethnicity in today's Russia, in H. Blakkisrud and P. Kolsto (eds) *Russia Before and After the Crimea: Nationalism and Identity, 2010–17*, Edinburgh: Edinburgh University Press, pp. 258–81.

Goodwin, M. and Milazzo, C. (2017) Taking back control? Investigating the role of immigration in the 2016 vote for Brexit. *The British Journal of Politics and International Relations*, 19(3): 450–64.

Goren, H. and Yemini, M. (2017) Global citizenship education redefined: A systematic review of empirical studies on global citizenship education. *International Journal of Educational Research*, 82: 170–83.

Greater London Authority (2018) *The Mayor's Strategy for Social Inclusion*. London: Greater London Authority.

Green, A., Janmaat, G. and Han, C. (2009) *Regimes of Social Cohesion*. Institute of Education, University of London.

Gustavsson, G. (2015) Liberal national identity: thinner than conservative, thicker than civic – but in terms of what? Paper presented at the European Consortium for Political Research Joint Sessions, Warsaw. Available at https://ecpr.eu/Filestore/PaperProposal/c80bd0a3-8bbd-455e-9b28-0e2bab9acc70.pdf [Accessed 9 May 2019].

Habib, S. (2018) *Learning and Teaching British Values: Policies and Perspectives on British Identities*. London: Palgrave Macmillan.

Haylett, C. (2001) Illegitimate subjects? Abject Whites, neoliberal modernisation, and middle-class multiculturalism. *Environment and Planning D: Society and Space*, 19(3): 351–70.

Healy, M. (2018) Belonging, social cohesion and fundamental British Values. *British Journal of Educational Studies*, doi: 10.1080/00071005.2018.1506091.

Hess, D. (2004) Controversies about controversial issues in democratic education. *PS: Political Science & Politics*, 37(2): 257–61.

Ho, L. (2018) Conceptions of global citizenship education in East and South-East Asia, in in I. Davies, L.C. Ho, D. Kiwan, C.L. Peck, A. Peterson, E. Sant and Y. Waghid (eds) *The Palgrave Handbook of Global Citizenship and Education*, London: Palgrave Macmillan, pp. 83–95.

Holmwood, J. and O'Toole, T. (2018) *Countering Extremism in British Schools?* Bristol: Policy Press.

Home Office (2013) *Life in the United Kingdom: A Guide for New Residents* (3rd edn). London: The Stationery Office. Available at https://lifeintheuktestweb.co.uk/the-values-and-principles-of-the-uk/ [Accessed 9 May 2019].

Home Office (2015) *Revised Prevent Duty Guidance for England and Wales*. London: Home Office. Available at https://www.gov.uk/government/publications/prevent-duty-guidance [Accessed 9 May 2019].

Home Office (2018a) *Individuals Referred to and Supported Through the Prevent Programme, April 2016 to March 2017*. Statistical Bulletin 06/18. London: Home Office. Available at https://assets.publishing.service.gov.uk/government/uploads/system/uploads/attachment_data/file/694002/individuals-referred-supported-prevent-programme-apr2016-mar2017.pdf [Accessed 9 May 2019].

Home Office (2018b) *Hate Crime, England and Wales, 2017/18*. Statistical Bulletin 20/18. London: Home Office. Available at https://assets.publishing.service.gov.uk/government/uploads/system/uploads/attachment_data/file/748598/hate-crime-1718-hosb2018.pdf [Accessed 9 May 2019].

Home Office (2018c) *Individuals Referred to and Supported Through the Prevent Programme, April 2017 to March 2018*. Statistical Bulletin 31/18. London: Home Office.

Home Office (2018d) Counter-terrorism Strategy: CONTEST 2018. London: Home Office.

Honig, B. (2001) *Democracy and the Foreigner*. Princeton: Princeton University Press.

Horton, J. (1996) Toleration as a virtue, in D. Heyd (ed.) *Toleration*, Princeton: Princeton University Press, pp. 28–43.

House of Lords Select Committee on Citizenship and Civic Engagement (2018) *The Ties that Bind: Citizenship and Civic Engagement in the 21st Century*. London: House of Lords.

Hung, R. (2010) In search of affective citizenship. *Policy Futures in Education*, 8(5): 488–98.

Hunter, I. (1994) *Rethinking the School: Subjectivity, Bureaucracy, Criticism*. Sydney: Allen & Unwin.

Hunter, S. (2015) *Power, Politics and the Emotions*. London: Routledge.

Isin, E. (2004) The neurotic citizen. *Citizenship Studies*, 8(3): 217–35.

Jackson, E. and Benson, M. (2014), Neither 'deepest, darkest Peckham' nor 'run-of-the-Mill' East Dulwich: The middle classes and their 'others' in an inner-London neighbourhood. *International Journal of Urban and Regional Research*, 38(4): 1195–210.

James, J. (2018) Mobilising Republican values in the 'post-Charlie' context. Paper presented at conference on Community, Citizenship and Cohesion: Schools and the Promotion of 'Fundamental British Values', 29 November, UCL Institute of Education.

James, J. (forthcoming) An Investigation into the Impact of Islamist Terrorism on Education Policy and Practice in England and France'. Doctoral thesis, UCL Institute of Education.

Janmaat, G. (2018) Educational influences on young people's support for fundamental British values. *British Educational Research Journal*, 44(2): 251–73.

Jensen, K.K. and Mouritsen, P. (2015) The politics of citizenship education in Denmark. Paper presented at the 43rd ECPR Conference, University of Warsaw.

Jensen, K.K. and Mouritsen, P. (2017) Nationalism in a liberal register: beyond the 'paradox of universalism' in immigrant integration politics. *British Journal of Political Science* [online], pp. 1–20.

Jerome, L. and Clemitshaw G. (2012) Teaching (about) Britishness? An investigation into trainee teachers' understanding of Britishness in relation to citizenship and the discourse of civic nationalism. *The Curriculum Journal*, 23(1): 19–41.

Jerome, L. and Elwick, A. (2017) Identifying an educational response to the prevent policy: student perspectives on learning about terrorism, extremism and radicalisation. *British Journal of Educational Studies*, 67(1): 97–114.

Johnson, C. (2010) The politics of affective citizenship: from Blair to Obama. *Citizenship Studies*, 14(5): 495–509.

Johnson, L. and Morris, P. (2010) Towards a framework for critical citizenship education. *The Curriculum Journal*, 21(1): 77–96.

Joiko, S. (2019, forthcoming) *The schooling experience of Latin American migrant families in Chilean schools.* PhD thesis, Institute of Education, UCL.

Joint Committee on Human Rights (2017) *Counter-Extremism: Second Part of the 2016–17 Session.* London: Houses of Parliament.

Jones, R. and Merriman, P. (2009) Hot, banal, and everyday nationalism: bilingual road signs in Wales. *Political Geography*, 28(3): 164–73.

Joppke, C. (2004) The retreat of multiculturalism in the liberal state: theory and policy. *The British Journal of Sociology*, 55(2): 237–57.

Joppke, C. (2007) Beyond national models: Civic integration policies for immigrants in Western Europe. *West European Politics*, 30(1): 1–22.

Joppke, C. (2010) The inevitable lightening of citizenship. *European Journal of Sociology/Archives Européennes de Sociologie*, 51(1): 9–32.

Joseph, J. (2013) Resilience as embedded neoliberalism: a governmentality approach. *Resilience*, 1(1): 38–52.

Joshee, R. and Sinfield, I. (2010) The Canadian multicultural education policy web: lessons to learn, pitfalls to avoid. *Multicultural Education Review*, 2(1): 55–75.

Jubilee Centre for Character and Virtues (Jubilee Centre) (2017) *A Framework for Character Education in Schools*. Available at https://uobschool.org.uk/wp-content/uploads/2017/08/Framework-for-Character-Education-2017-Jubilee-Centre.pdf [Accessed 9 May 2019].

Katwala, S. (2018) This young diverse football team is one that everybody in modern England can be proud of. Available at https://inews.co.uk/sport/football/world-cup/england-world-cup-2018-squad-diversity [Accessed 9 May 2019].

Keating, A. and Benton, T. (2013) Creating cohesive citizens in England? Exploring the role of diversity, deprivation and democratic climate at school. *Education, Citizenship and Social Justice*, 8(2): 165–84.

Keddie, A. (2014) The politics of Britishness: multiculturalism, schooling and social cohesion. *British Educational Research Journal*, 40(3): 539–54.

Keddie, A. (2017) Primary school leadership in England: performativity and matters of professionalism. *British Journal of Sociology of Education*, 38(8): 1245–57.

Keddie, A. (2018) Supporting disadvantaged students in an English primary school: matters of entrepreneurial and traditional professionalism. *Cambridge Journal of Education,* 48(2): 197–212.

Kerr, D. (2018) The Crick Report and the wisdom of hindsight. *Teaching Citizenship*, 47: 12–17.

Kibble, D. (1998) Moral education dilemmas for the teacher. *Curriculum Journal*, 9(1): 51–61.

Kisby, B. (2017). 'Politics is ethics done in public': exploring linkages and disjunctions between citizenship education and character education in England. *Journal of Social Science Education*, 16(3): 1–21.

Kiwan, D. (2018) The Middle East, in I. Davies, L.C. Ho, D. Kiwan, C.L. Peck, A. Peterson, E. Sant and Y. Waghid (eds) *The Palgrave Handbook of Global Citizenship and Education*, London: Palgrave Macmillan, pp. 37–50.

Koch, N. and Paasi, A. (2016) Banal nationalism 20 years on: re-thinking, re-formulating and re-contextualizing the concept. *Political Geography*, 54: 1–6.

Kofman E. (2005) Citizenship, migration and the reassertion of national identity, *Citizenship Studies*, 9(5): 453–67.

Kohn, H. (1965) *Nationalism, Its Meaning and History* (rev. edn). Princeton: Van Nostrand.

Korteweg, A.C. and Triadafilopoulos, T. (2015) Is multiculturalism dead? Groups, governments and the 'real work of integration'. *Ethnic and Racial Studies*, 38(5): 663–80.

Kostakopoulou, D. (2006) Thick, thin and thinner patriotisms: is this all there is? *Oxford Journal of Legal Studies*, 26(1): 73–106.

Kostakopoulou, D. (2010) The anatomy of civic integration. *The Modern Law Review*, 73(6): 933–58.

Kulz, C. (2017) *Factories for Learning: Making Race, Class and Inequality in the Neoliberal Academy*. Oxford: Oxford University Press.

Kymlicka, W. (2007) *Multicultural Odysseys: Navigating the New International Politics of Diversity* [on demand]. Oxford: Oxford University Press.

Kymlicka, W. (2015) Solidarity in diverse societies: beyond neoliberal multiculturalism and welfare chauvinism. *Comparative Migration Studies*, 3(17): 1–19.

Lander, V., Elton-Chalcraft, S. and Revell, L. (2016) Introduction to fundamental British values. *Journal of Education for Teaching*, 42(3): 274–9.

Lentin, A. (2014) Post-race, post politics: the paradoxical rise of culture after multiculturalism. *Ethnic and Racial Studies*, 37(8): 1268–85.

Levey, G.B. (2014) Liberal nationalism and the Australian citizenship tests. *Citizenship Studies*, 18(2): 175–89.

Lewis, H. and Craig, G. (2014) 'Multiculturalism is never talked about': community cohesion and local policy contradictions in England. *Policy & Politics*, 42(1): 21–38.

Lipsky, M. (1983) *Street-Level Bureaucracy*. New York: Russell Sage Foundation.

Long, R. (2016) *Religious Education in Schools (England)*. Briefing Paper CBP-7167. London: House of Commons Library.

Long, R. (2018) *Counter-Extremism Policy in English Schools*. Briefing Paper CBP-7345. London: House of Commons Library.

Lott, T. (2017) British values for kids? Scepticism and bloody-mindedness would be a good start. *The Guardian*, 17 September.

Mac an Ghaill, M. and Haywood, C. (2017) Educating Muslim students, in M. Mac an Ghaill and C. Haywood (eds) *Muslim Students, Education and Neoliberalism*. London: Palgrave Macmillan, pp. 199–215.

Macaluso, A. (2016) *From Countering to Preventing Radicalization Through Education: Limits and Opportunities*. The Hague Institute for Global Justice Working Paper, 18.

Markell, P. (2000) Making affect safe for democracy? On 'constitutional patriotism'. *Political Theory*, 28(1): 38–63.

Mason, A. (2018) The critique of multiculturalism in Britain: integration, separation, and shared identification. *Critical Review of International Social and Political Philosophy*, 21(1): 22–45.

Mathieu, F. (2018) The failure of state multiculturalism in the UK? An analysis of the UK's multicultural policy for 2000–2015. *Ethnicities*, 18(1): 43–69.

Maxwell, C. and Aggleton P. (2013) Introduction: Privilege, agency and affect – understanding the production and effects of action, in C. Maxwell & P. Aggleton (eds) *Privilege, Agency and Affect*. Basingstoke. Palgrave Macmillan.

Maylor, U. (2014) Promoting British values opens up a can of worms for teachers. *The Guardian*, 12 June.

McCuaig, L. (2012) Dangerous carers: pastoral power and the caring teacher of contemporary Australian schooling. *Educational Philosophy and Theory*, 44(8): 862–77.

McGhee, D. and Zhang, S. (2017) Nurturing resilient future citizens through value consistency vs. the retreat from multiculturalism and securitisation in the promotion of British values in schools in the UK. *Citizenship Studies*, 21(8): 937–50.

McIntosh, P. (1992) White privilege: Unpacking the invisible knapsack, in A. M. Filor (ed.) *Multiculturalism*, New York: New York State Council of Educational Institutions.

McLaughlin, T.H. (2000) Citizenship education in England: the Crick Report and beyond. *Journal of Philosophy of Education*, 34(4): 541–70.

Meer, N. (2010) *Citizenship, Identity and the Politics of Multiculturalism*. Basingstoke: Palgrave Macmillan.

Miah, S. (2017) The Muslim problematic: Muslims, state schools and security. *International Studies in Sociology of Education*, 26(2): 138–50.

Militz, E. and Schurr, C. (2016) Affective nationalism: banalities of belonging in Azerbaijan. *Political Geography*, 54: 54–63.

Miller, D. (1995) *On Nationalism*. Oxford: Clarendon Press.

Miller, D. (2000) *Citizenship and National Identity*. Cambridge: Polity Press.

Miller, D. and Ali, S. (2014) Testing the national identity argument. *European Political Science Review*, 6(2): 237–59.

Ministere de l'Education Nationale (2018) *La Laicite a l'Ecole*. Available at http://91.snuipp.fr/IMG/pdf/vademecum_laicite_vf2_955894_2018-06-09_18-42-3_763.pdf [Accessed 9 May 2019].

Ministry for Housing, Communities and Local Government (MHCLG) (2018a) *Government Response to the Lords Select Committee on Citizenship and Civic Engagement*. London: MHCLG.

Ministry of Housing, Communities and Local Government (MHCLG) (2018b) *Integrated Communities Strategy Green Paper: Building Stronger, More United Communities*. London: MHCLG.

Mitchell, K. (2003) Neoliberal governmentality in the European Union: education, training, and technologies of citizenship. *Environment and Planning D: Society and Space*, 24(3): 389–407.

Modood, T. (2013) *Multiculturalism: A Civic Idea* (2nd edn). Cambridge: Polity Press.

Moffatt, A. (2011) *No Outsiders in Our School*. London: Routledge.

Moncrieffe, M. and Moncrieffe, A. (2019) An examination of imagery used to represent fundamental British values and British identity on primary school display boards. *London Review of Education*, 17(1): 52–69.

Mookherjee, M. (2005) Affective citizenship: feminism, postcolonialism and the politics of recognition. *Critical Review of International Social and Political Philosophy*, 8(1): 31–50.

Moore, A. and Clarke, M. (2016) 'Cruel optimism': Teacher attachment to professionalism in an era of performativity. *Journal of Education Policy*, 31(5): 666–77.

Moore, A. (2018) *The Affected Teacher: Psychosocial Perspectives on Professional Experience and Policy Resistance*. London: Routledge.

Morey, O. and Yaqin, A. (2011) *Framing Muslims: Stereotyping and Representation after 9/11*. Cambridge, MA: Harvard University Press.

Moulin, D. (2012) Religious education in England after 9/11. *Religious Education*, 107(2): 158–73.

Mouritsen, P. and Jaeger, A. (2018) *Designing Civic Education for Diverse Societies: Models, Tradeoffs, and Outcomes*. Brussels: Migration Policy Institute Europe.

Muir, H. (2018) How England's World Cup progress gives us a shot at a hopeful future. Available at https://www.theguardian.com/commentisfree/2018/jul/11/england-world-cup-diverse-english-football-team [Accessed 9 May 2019].

Müller, J.W. (2007) A general theory of constitutional patriotism. *International Journal of Constitutional Law*, 6(1): 72–95.

National Police Chiefs Council (2017) Latest hate crime figures covering the priod of 2017 UK terrorist attacks published. Available at https://news.npcc.police.uk/releases/latest-hate-crime-figures-covering-the-period-of-2017-uk-terrorist-attacks-published [Accessed 29 April 2019].

Neal S., Bennett, K., Cochrane, A. and Mohan, G. (2018) *The Lived Experiences of Multiculture: The New Spatial and Social Relations of Diversity*. London: Routledge.

Nettleton, S. (1997) Governing the risky self: how to become healthy, wealthy and wise, in A. Petersen and R. Bunton (eds) *Foucault, Health and Medicine*, Abingdon: Routledge.

Novelli, M. (2017) Education and countering violent extremism: western logics from south to north? *Compare: A Journal of Comparative and International Education*, 47(6): 835–51.

Noyes, A. (2005) Pupil voice: purpose, power and the possibilities of democratic schooling. *British Educational Research Journal*, 31(4): 533–40.

Nye, P. (2014) Inspections reveal Ofsted's approach to British values in wake of 'Trojan Horse'. *Schools Week*, 27 November.

O'Donnell, A. (2016) Securitisation, counterterrorism and the silencing of dissent: the educational implications of Prevent. *British Journal of Educational Studies*, 64(1): 53–76.

O'Donnell, A. (2017) Pedagogical injustice and counter-terrorist education. *Education, Citizenship and Social Justice*, 12(2): 177–93.

O'Neill, A. (2017), *Hate Crimes, England and Wales 2016/17*. Statistical Bulletin 17/17. London: Home Office.

Ofsted (2019) *School Inspection Handbook*. Manchester, Ofsted.

Open Society Justice Initiative (2016) *Eroding Trust: The UK's Prevent Counter-Extremism Strategy in Health and Education*. New York: Open Society Foundations.

Osler, A. (2000) The Crick Report: difference, equality and racial justice. *Curriculum Journal*, 11(1): 25–37.

Osler, A. (2011) Teacher interpretations of citizenship education: national identity, cosmopolitan ideals, and political realities. *Journal of Curriculum Studies*, 43(1): 1–24.

Osler, A. and Starkey, H. (2018) Extending the theory and practice of education for cosmopolitan citizenship. *Educational Review*, 70(1): 31–40.

O'Toole, T., Meer, N., DeHanas, D.N., Jones, S.H. and Modood, T. (2016) Governing through Prevent? *Sociology*, 50(1): 160–77.

Oulton, C., Day, V., Dillon J. and Grace M. (2004) Controversial issues – teachers' attitudes and practices in the context of citizenship education. *Oxford Review of Education*, 30(4): 489–507.

REFERENCES

Oxley, L. and Morris, P. (2013) Global citizenship: a typology for distinguishing its multiple conceptions. *British Journal of Educational Studies*, 61(3): 301–25.

Ozkirimli, U. (2017) *Theories of Nationalism* (3rd edn). London: Palgrave Macmillan.

Pais, A. and Costa, M. (2017) An ideology critique of global citizenship education. *Critical Studies in Education* [online], 1–16.

Panjwani, F., (2016) Towards an overlapping consensus: Muslim teachers' views on fundamental British values. *Journal of Education for Teaching*, 42, 3: 329–40.

Panjwani, F., Revell, L., Gholami, R. and Diboll, M. (eds) (2018) *Education and Extremisms*. London: Routledge.

Peck C. and Pashby, K. (2018) Global citizenship education in North America, in I. Davies, L.C. Ho, D. Kiwan, C.L. Peck, A. Peterson, E. Sant and Y. Waghid (eds) *The Palgrave Handbook of Global Citizenship and Education*, London: Palgrave Macmillan, pp. 51–65.

Peterson A., Miligan, A. and Wood, B. (2018) Global citizenship education in Australasia, in I. Davies, L.C. Ho, D. Kiwan, C.L. Peck, A. Peterson, E. Sant and Y. Waghid (eds) *The Palgrave Handbook of Global Citizenship and Education*, London: Palgrave Macmillan, pp. 3–20.

Phillips, C., Tse, D. and Johnson, F. (2011) *Community Cohesion and PREVENT: How Have Schools Responded?* Research Report DFE-RR085. London: Department for Education.

Phillips, D. (2006) Parallel lives? Challenging discourses of British Muslim Self-Segregation. *Environment and Planning D: Society and Space*, 24(1): 25–40.

Pykett, J. (2007) Making citizens governable? The Crick Report as governmental technology. *Journal of Education Policy*, 22(3): 301–19.

Pykett, J., Saward, M. and Schaefer, A. (2010) Framing the good citizen. *The British Journal of Politics and International Relations*, 12(4): 523–38.

Qualifications and Curriculum Authority (QCA) (1998) *Education for Citizenship and the Teaching of Democracy in Schools: Final Report of the Advisory Group on Citizenship* (The Crick Report). London: QCA.

Qualifications and Curriculum Authority (QCA) (2004) *Religious Education: The Non-Statutory National Framework*. London: QCA.

Quartermaine A. (2016) Discussing terrorism: a pupil-inspired guide to UK counter-terrorism policy implementation in religious education classrooms in England. *British Journal of Religious Education*, 38(1): 13–29.

Quartermaine, A. (2017) The disposition of concern: an exploration into the affects of the power–knowledge dynamics uncovered during research into pupils' perceptions of terrorism. *International Journal of Research & Method in Education*, 40(5): 541–53.

Ragazzi, F. (2017) *Students as Suspects?* Strasbourg: Council of Europe.

Reay, D. (2017) *Miseducation*. Bristol: Policy Press.

Revell, L. (2018) Resilience and soft power, in F. Panjwani, L. Revell, R. Gholami, and M. Diboll (eds) *Education and Extremisms*, London: Routledge, pp. 191–203.

Revell, L. and Bryan H. (2018) *Fundamental British Values in Education: Radicalisation, National Identity and Britishness*. Bingley: Emerald Publishing.

Richardson, R. and Bolloten, B. (2014) 'Fundamental British Values': origins, controversy, ways forward: a symposium. *Race Equality Teaching*, 32(3): 9–20.

Richardson, R. and Bolloten, B. (2015) *The Great British Values Disaster: Education, Security and Vitriolic Hate*. London: Institute of Race Relations.

Rizvi, F. and Lingard, B. (2009) *Globalizing Education Policy*. London: Routledge.

Rollock, N., Gillborn, D., Vincent, C., and Ball, S. (2015) *The Colour of Class*. London: Routledge.

Rosen, M. (2014) What's so 'British' about your 'British values'? *The Guardian*, 1 July.

Rowe, D., Horsely, N., Breslin, T. and Thorpe, T. (2012) Benefit or burden? How English schools responded to the duty to promote community cohesion. *Journal of Social Science Education*, 11(3): 88–107.

Saeed, T. (2018) Education and disengagement: extremism and the perception of Muslim students, in F. Panjwani, L. Revell, R. Gholami and M. Diboll (eds) *Education and Extremisms*, London: Routledge, pp. 45–59.

Sant, E. and Gonzalez Valencia, G. (2018) Global citizenship education in Latin America, in I. Davies, L.C. Ho, D. Kiwan, C.L. Peck, A. Peterson, E. Sant and Y. Waghid (eds) *The Palgrave Handbook of Global Citizenship and Education*, London: Palgrave Macmillan, pp. 67–82.

Sant, E. and Hanley, C. (2018) Political assumptions underlying pedagogies of national education: the case of student teachers teaching 'British values' in England. *British Educational Research Journal*, 44(2): 319–37.

Sant, E., McDonnell, J., Menendez Alvarez-Hevia, D., Pashby, K., Hanley, C. and Thiel, J. (2017) Pedagogies of agonistic democracy and global citizenship education. Available at https://e-space.mmu.ac.uk/619751 [Accessed 29 April 2019].

Sant, E., Davies, I., Pashby, K. and Shultz, L. (2018) *Global Citizenship Education*. London: Bloomsbury.

Scanlon, T. (2003) *The Difficulty of Tolerance: Essays in Political Philosophy*. Cambridge: Cambridge University Press.

Shackle, S. (2017) Trojan Horse: the real story behind the fake 'Islamic plot' to take over schools. *The Guardian*, 1 September. Available at https://www.theguardian.com/world/2017/sep/01/trojan-horse-the-real-story-behind-the-fake-islamic-plot-to-take-over-schools [Accessed 9 May 2019].

Shotwell, A. (2011) *Knowing Otherwise: Race, Gender, and Implicit Understanding*. University Park: Pennsylvania State University Press.

Silk, M. (2011) Towards a sociological analysis of London 2012. *Sociology*, 45(5): 733–48.

Singh, P., Thomas, S. and Harris, J. (2013) Recontextualising policy discourses: a Bernsteinian perspective on policy interpretation, translation, enactment. *Journal of Education Policy*, 28(4): 465–80.

Skey, M. and Antonisch, M. (2017) Conclusion: the present and future of nationalism, in *Everyday Nationhood: Theorising Culture, Identity and Belonging after Banal Nationalism*, London: Palgrave Macmillan pp. 323–34.

Smith, A. (2000) *The Nation in History: Historiographical Debates about Ethnicity and Nationalism*. Oxford: Polity Press.

Smith, R.M. (2010) On the limits of light citizenship: Christian Joppke, *Citizenship and Immigration* (Cambridge, Polity Press, 2010). *European Journal of Sociology*, 51(3): 547–50.

Soutphommasane, T. (2012) *The Virtuous Citizen: Patriotism in a Multicultural Society*. Cambridge: Cambridge University Press.

Spielman, A. (2017) Amanda Spielman's speech at the Birmingham Education Partnership conference, 22 September. Available at https://www.gov.uk/government/speeches/amanda-spielmans-speech-at-the-birmingham-school-partnership-conference [Accessed 29 April 2019].

Spielman, A. (2018a) Amanda Spielman's speech at the Church of England Foundation for Educational Leadership, 1 February. Available at https://www.gov.uk/government/speeches/amanda-spielmans-speech-at-the-church-of-england-foundation-for-education-leadership [Accessed 9 May 2019].

Spielman, A. (2018b) Amanda Spielman's speech to the Policy Exchange think tank: The ties that bind, 9 July. Available at https://www.gov.uk/government/speeches/amanda-spielmans-speech-to-the-policy-exchange-think-tank [Accessed 9 May 2019].

Starkey, H. (2018) Fundamental British values and citizenship education: tensions between national and global perspectives. *Geografiska Annaler: Series B, Human Geography*, 100(2): 149–62.

Stradling, R. (1985) Controversial issues in the curriculum. *Bulletin of Environmental Education*, 170: 9–13.

Strandbrink, P. (2017) *Civic Education and Liberal Democracy*. London: Palgrave Macmillan.

Struthers, A. (2017) Teaching British values in our schools: but why not human rights values? *Social & Legal Studies*, 26(1): 89–110.

Suissa, J. (2015) Character education and the disappearance of the political. *Ethics and Education*, 10(1): 105–17.

Sukarieh, M. and Tannock, S. (2016) The deradicalisation of education: terror, youth and the assault on learning. *Race & Class,* 57(4): 22–38.

Sukarieh, M. and Tannock, S. (2018) The global securitisation of youth. *Third World Quarterly*, 39(5): 854–70.

Sung, Y.K., Park, M. and Choi, I.S. (2013) National construction of global education: a critical review of the national curriculum standards for South Korean global high schools. *Asia Pacific Education Review*, 14(3): 285–94.

Suvarierol, S. (2012) Nation-freezing: images of the nation and the migrant in citizenship packages. *Nations and Nationalism*, 18(2): 210–29.

Tamir, Y. (1993) *Liberal Nationalism.* Princeton: Princeton University Press.

Tammi, T. and Rajala, A. (2018). Deliberative communication in elementary classroom meetings. *Scandinavian Journal of Educational Research*, 62(4): 617–30.

Taylor, C. (1994) The politics of recognition, in A. Gutmann (ed.) *Multiculturalism and the Politics of Recognition*, Princeton: Princeton University Press, pp. 25–74.

Taylor, S., Henry, M., Lingard, B. and Rizvi, F. (1997) *Educational Policy and the Politics of Change.* London: Routledge.

Teague, L. (2018) The curriculum as a site of counter politics: theorising the 'domain of the sayable'. *British Journal of Sociology of Education*, 39(1): 92–106.

Thomas, P. (2011) *Youth, Multiculturalism and Community Cohesion.* Basingstoke: Palgrave Macmillan.

Thomas, P. (2016) Youth, terrorism and education: Britain's Prevent programme. *International Journal of Lifelong Education*, 35(2): 171–87.

Thomas, P. (2017) Changing experiences of responsibilisation and contestation within counter-terrorism policies: the British Prevent experience. *Policy & Politics*, 45(3): 305–21.

Tomlinson, S. (2019) *Education and Race from Empire to Brexit*. Bristol: Policy Press.

Troyna, B. (1993) *Racism and Education*. Milton Keynes: Open University Press.

Tyler, I. (2010) Designed to fail: a biopolitics of British citizenship. *Citizenship Studies*, 14(1): 61–74.

Van Breugel, I. and Scholten, P. (2017) Mainstreaming in response to superdiversity? The governance of migration-related diversity in France, the UK and the Netherlands. *Policy & Politics*, 45(4): 511–26.

Vanderbeck, R. and Johnson, P. (2016) The promotion of British values: sexual orientation equality, religion, and England's schools. *International Journal of Law, Policy and the Family*, 30(3): 292–321.

Vincent, C. (2018) Civic virtue and values teaching in a 'post-secular' world. *Theory and Research in Education*, 16(2): 226–43.

Vincent, C. (2019) Cohesion, citizenship and coherence: schools' responses to the British values policy', *British Journal of Sociology of Education* 40(1): 17–32.

Vincent, C., Neal, S. and Iqbal, H. (2018) *Friendship and Diversity*. London: Palgrave Macmillan.

Walkerdine, V. and Jimenez, L. (2012) *Gender, work and community after de-industrialisation: A psychosocial approach to affect*. London: Palgrave Macmillan.

Waller, C. (2018) Things we forgot to remember. *Teaching Citizenship*, 47: 8–11.

Werbner, P. (2007) Veiled interventions in pure space: honour, shame and embodied struggles among Muslims in Britain and France. *Theory, Culture & Society*, 24(2): 161–86.

Wesselhoeft, K. (2017) On the 'front lines' of the classroom: moral education and Muslim students in French state schools. *Oxford Review of Education*, 43(5): 626–41.

Wetherell, M. (2014) *Affect and Emotion*. London: SAGE.

White, C., Gibb, J., Lea, J. and Street, C. (2017) *Developing Character Skills in Schools: Qualitative Case Studies: Final Report*. London: Department for Education.

REFERENCES

Whitty, G. and Wisby, E. (2007) Whose voice? An exploration of the current policy interest in pupil involvement in school decision-making. *International Studies in Sociology of Education*, 17(3): 303–19.

Wilkins, C. (2011) Professionalism and the post-performative teacher. *Professional Development in Education*, 37(3): 389–409.

Williams, R. (1961/2011) *The Long Revolution*. Cardigan: Parthian Books.

Williams, R. (1977) *Marxism and Literature*. Oxford: Oxford University Press.

Yack, B. (2014) Response to debate on Bernard Yack's book *Nationalism and the Moral Psychology of Community*. *Nations and Nationalism*, 20(3): 395–414.

Yemini, M., Goren, H. and Maxwell, C. (2018) Global citizenship education in the era of mobility, conflict and globalisation. *British Journal of Educational Studies* [online], 1–10.

Zembylas, M. (2002) 'Structures of feeling' in curriculum and teaching: theorizing the emotional rules. *Educational Theory*, 52(2): 187–208.

Zembylas, M. (2013a) Affective citizenship in multicultural societies: implications for critical citizenship education. *Citizenship Teaching & Learning*, 9(1): 5–18.

Zembylas, M. (2013b) The 'crisis of pity' and the radicalization of solidarity: toward critical pedagogies of compassion. *Educational Studies*, 49(6): 504–21.

Zembylas, M. (2015) 'Pedagogy of discomfort'and its ethical implications: the tensions of ethical violence in social justice education. *Ethics and Education*, 10(2): 163–74.

Zembylas, M. (2016a) Making sense of the complex entanglement between emotion and pedagogy: contributions of the affective turn. *Cultural Studies of Science Education*, 11: 539–50.

Zembylas, M. (2016b) The therapisation of social justice as an emotional regime: implications for critical education. *Journal of Professional Capital and Community*, 1(4): 286–301.

Zembylas, M. (2017) Wilful ignorance and the emotional regime of schools. *British Journal of Educational Studies*, 65(4): 499–515.

Index

see also Prevent strategy
Counter-Terrorism and Security
  Act 2015 16
counter-terrorism strategies 8, 116
Cowden, S. 16
Crick Report 44, 109
'critical pedagogy' 144
'cultural difference' 55
cultural racism 11
curriculum, narrowing of 38

D

'dangerous conversations' 106,
  107–12, 130
Davies, L. 38, 121
De Wilde, M. 43
Dembe (teacher-respondent),
  Kenton Secondary School
  100, 119
democracy (FBV) 1, 53, 69
  and school councils 79, 80, 81–5,
  92–3, 147
Denise (teacher-respondent),
  Moreton Grange Secondary
  Academy 100
Denmark 36, 39
Department of Education 106
Diane (headteacher-respondent),
  Shire Primary School 78–9,
  99, 130
'difference-conscious' policies 12
Dill, J. 143
'dirty' issues 108
Disability Rights Commission
  23n6
disappointment, emotional
  responses to 87–8
diversity 12–13, 38
  ambiguity concerning 54–5
'domain of the sayable' 111, 128
Dominic (teacher-respondent),
  Valley High Secondary
  School 126
Don (teacher-respondent), Downs
  Secondary Academy 109, 110,
  112–13, 124
Downs Secondary Academy 1, 61,
  65, 126, 140

Engagement with FBV 109, 110,
  113, 116, 117
lessons on terrorism 116, 117
profile 63
Repackaging FBV 80
Representing Britain 71
teachers' attitudes and responses
  71, 102, 103, 104–5, 109, 110,
  112–13, 124, 140
Duyvendak, J. 43

E

East Heath Secondary School
  profile 64
  teachers' attitudes and
  responses 125
Eastern Europe, migration from 6
EBacc (English Baccalaureate)
  57–8, 104, 137
Ecclestone, K. 88
'economic nationalism' 37–8
Edelman, M.J. 69
Education Act 1996 108
educational policy and context in
  England 3, 56–8, 96
Eliot, T.S. 69
Elliott (headteacher-respondent),
  Marina Grammar School 119–20
Elwick, A. 106
EMC *(Enseignement moral et civique),*
  France 39–40
emotional intelligence 88–9
emotions 48n1
  'correct' emotions, and citizenship
  education 41–3
  see also affective citizenship
Engagement with FBV 3, 70, 95,
  106–7, 138, 141–2
  and 'dangerous conversations' 106,
  107–12, 130
  discussing terrorism 116–21
  and 'pedagogies of
  discomfort' 114–16
  strategies for 112–14
England
  citizenship education 44–7
  educational policy and context 3,
  56–8, 96